"We have four operating units across which we leverage Sandler Training, which provides us with a common process and common language. That's important as we think about transferring talent and leadership between our businesses. Sonoco's emphasis on strategic account management and sustainable value creation are completely aligned with the Sandler Enterprise Selling (SES) process and its tools. I believe that some of our greatest potential and greatest assets are to be found in our relationships with our existing customers. I'm excited about our growth prospects as we work the SES process and tools to unlock this potential."

—Greg L. Powell, Vice President, Sonoco Protective
Solutions—Packaging and Components

"We've been using the Sandler methods for many years. We chose the Sandler Enterprise Selling program because it takes our skills to the level necessary for us to outperform our competition in a highly competitive, highly sophisticated market."

—Ken Harris, Vice President, Sales and Marketing,
Pelstar LLC/Health-o-meter® Professional Scales

"Why use Sandler Enterprise Selling? For DS Smith Plastics, the answer has been obvious—it's given us a common set of tools for progressing a sale to close, a common language to use when in the process of making that sale, and above all else a common strategic platform to make the process scalable and repeatable. Sandler Enterprise Selling takes the well proven Sandler principles to the next level and can really drive meaningful change within your organization."

—Kevin Grogan, President, DS Smith Plastics North America

SANDLER ENTERPRISE SELLING

WINNING, GROWING, AND RETAINING MAJOR ACCOUNTS

DAVID H. MATTSON
BRIAN W. SULLIVAN

New York Chicago San Francisco Athens London Madrid
Mexico City Milan New Delhi Singapore Sydney Toronto

This book is dedicated to David H. Sandler, who created the definitive professional selling system. It continues to be implemented all over the world by the global network of Sandler trainers, who focus every day on helping clients improve and thrive. We are continually amazed at the enduring positive impact of their work, and his system, on livelihoods and lives in all industries.

Acknowledgments

Grateful thanks to Yusuf Toropov and all those at the Sandler Home Office who dedicated their time and expertise to this project.

Contents

CONTENTS

READ THIS FIRST

Frequently Asked Questions About Sandler Enterprise Selling

What Is Enterprise Selling?

When we use the phrase "enterprise selling" in this book, we mean selling into organizations that present any of the following challenges to the selling team: extended sales cycles; sophisticated competition; significant financial investment in pursuits; cross-functional teams; a focus on long-term business value rather than short-term pricing; wide, diverse buyer networks; complex decision structures; and a highly diversified organization and footprint.

Let's look at each of these elements individually.

- **Extended sales cycles.** When you are selling to enterprise clients, sales cycles can take months—sometimes years.
- **Sophisticated competition.** Your competition for enterprise business is likely to be sophisticated, strategically focused, and relentless. They come prepared!
- **Significant financial investment.** Pursuing an enterprise client requires a significant financial commitment as well as human, managerial, and logistical resources—not to mention the opportunity cost of not pursuing other business.
- **Cross-functional teams.** Because buyer networks of enterprise clients encompass many functions, so should your sales team. Positioning corresponding representatives on your team will show the strength and substance that enterprise clients demand.
- **Focus on long-term business value.** With the enterprise client, the business value of the solution to develop and implement must be unassailable or winning the business will be impossible.
- **Wide, diverse buyer networks.** The buying centers of enterprise clients are composed of a wide variety of functions, including purchasing, accounting, marketing, and legal. This, without question, makes the sales process more complex.
- **Complex decision structures.** In traditional selling, decisions are typically made quickly and based on price versus performance. In the enterprise world, however, the decision process can be complex, multi-layered and lengthy.

- **Diversified organization and footprint.** Enterprise clients differ from small business entities in their complex structures, multiple business lines, complexity of portfolios, depth, and breadth of markets served and globalization issues.

Enterprise selling is to traditional selling as chess is to checkers. Competitively pursuing large, complex accounts with multiple constituencies and multiple decision makers—to say nothing of winning and growing such accounts—is one of the biggest challenges for sales teams. Each of these pursuits represents a significant investment of the selling company's human, financial, management, and logistical resources. In order to maximize those investments, multiple parts of the selling organization must work together seamlessly. The business value of the proposed solutions they identify, develop, and implement must be unassailable because the competition is likely to be well-prepared, sophisticated, and relentless.

WHAT'S IT MEAN?

When we use the word account *in this book, we're referring to either a current or a prospective enterprise client.*

What Is Sandler Enterprise Selling?

The Sandler Enterprise Selling (SES) program, based on the proprietary Sandler Selling System® methodology created by David H. Sandler, provides a practical six-stage approach for winning business with profitable enterprise clients, serving them effectively, and expanding the relationships over time.

SES is a comprehensive, reinforcement-driven live training program designed specifically for selling teams committed to high achievement in the enterprise environment. This book is a preview of the program, not a substitute for it. In this program, we've taken everything that's made our training so effective over the past five decades and elevated it to address the unique needs of organizations selling to enterprise clients.

At Sandler Training, we've spent over 40 years helping companies around the world improve their sales processes to increase revenue and maximize profitability. What's driven their success is our scientific, methodical, and proven approach to selling. Our approach in SES, as in all of our programs, doesn't rely on quick fixes. Instead, it uses reinforcement to encourage incremental change over time to create lasting success.

Is SES Different from the Sandler Submarine?

No. It's an extension of it.

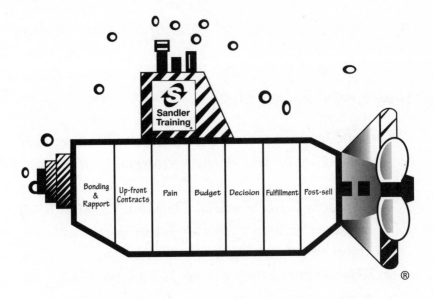

In a traditional sale—a sale that closes in a relatively short period of time and has a straightforward decision-making process—the proven model for success has been, for decades, the Sandler Submarine.

This selling model begins with the establishment of Bonding & Rapport and the setting of an Up-front Contract between seller and buyer. It moves through clear mutual assessments of Pain, Budget, and the Decision process, which, ideally, ends with the Fulfillment and Post-sell steps, where the buying agreement is finalized.

All of this is relevant to, and part of, the enterprise sale. But many additional variables enter the picture in these more complex selling situations. In the enterprise selling model, there are important things that must happen before Bonding & Rapport and after Post-Sell. Not only that: everything between those two events carries with it both logistical and political complexity in the enterprise arena. SES addresses all these variables, without changing any of the core Sandler principles.

How Is SES Structured?

SES is based on six highly strategic stages offering a continuous process of attaining, serving, and growing an enterprise account.

1. **Territory & Account Planning.** In this critical stage, you set a strong baseline for success though comprehensive planning.

2. **Opportunity Identification.** Next you analyze, assess, and initiate interaction on your most promising opportunities with the highest probability of success.

3. **Qualification.** Here you execute a practical plan to engage with the enterprise buyers to clarify the key opportunity parameters, which will improve and reinforce your position.

4. **Solution Development.** Now you craft a compelling solution directly addressing the needs and pains of the enterprise and its most influential executives.

5. **Proposing & Advancement.** It's time to finalize and deliver your client-focused solution and act on the resulting decision to achieve advancement.

6. **Service Delivery.** With the business relationship active, service delivery becomes critical: you coordinate team activities to maximize client satisfaction and grow the account.

The six interior puzzle pieces below represent the six interlocking stages of the SES process. Each of the stages is the focus of a main section of this book. Mastery of all six stages, via the live SES program and training that this book previews, is essential to competing and winning in this demanding selling arena.

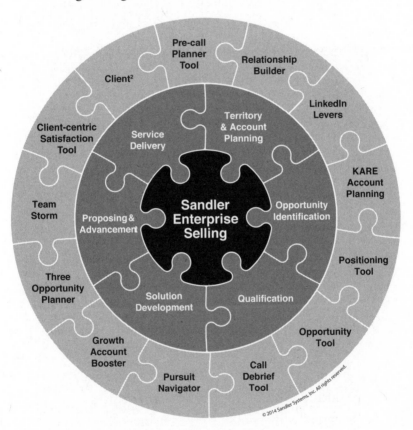

While SES is explained with six sequential steps, in practice it's a continuous cycle of ongoing selling to enterprise clients, serving them well and growing the business through streams of transactions over time.

What's in That Outer Ring?

SES offers 13 powerful tools integral to the strategic SES stages, designed to deliver a serious competitive edge.

1. **KARE Account Planning Tool:** Empowers your sales process by delivering value in territory and account planning as a customized profiling tool for both current clients and prospects; also creates a common organizational lexicon and facilitates comprehensive account understanding.

2. **Growth Account Booster Tool:** Drives collaborative development of a targeted growth plan involving the sales, operational, and delivery teams.

3. **LinkedIn® Levers Tool:** Takes research up a notch by allowing you to easily access critical information on individual client contacts and accounts as a whole using LinkedIn, the gold standard for research on people and businesses.

4. **Relationship Builder Tool:** Provides a simple baseline to chart an account's key decision makers and their personal goals; also identifies next steps to help enhance your relationship with each.

5. **Three Opportunity Planner Tool:** Ensures that focus is given to the highest probability short-term deals that position your organization for future business growth and profitability.

6. **Positioning Tool:** Identifies key buyers, your product/service's value propositions, and those of your primary competitors.

7. **Pre-call Planner Tool:** Helps you maximize the potential of an upcoming call with a simple set of steps guiding you through prebriefing and preparation of both questions and answers.

8. **Call Debrief Tool:** Helps you discover valuable lessons learned from a just-occurred sales call, including information learned, next steps planned, red flags identified, and more; also acts as a vehicle for sharing information across the selling team, especially important for members not on the call.

9. **Opportunity Tool:** Provides up-to-date snapshots of three critical aspects of an emerging deal—the competitors, the client's key pains, and the relevant applications; also provides action-oriented next steps.

10. **Pursuit Navigator Tool:** Brings together functional entities from across the selling organization to help drive Go/No-Go decisions regarding pursuits.

11. **Client-centric Satisfaction Tool:** Provides keen insights through a customized client satisfaction process designed to increase the probability of successful delivery and account expansion.

12. **Team Storm Tool:** Brings all client-serving elements together to work a problem or opportunity via a rapid team brainstorming process.

13. **Client^2 Tool:** Enables the sales and delivery teams to grow enterprise client marketplaces by following a logical framework of activities; also provides guidance in identifying opportunity areas.

In What Industries Have These Principles Delivered Results?

Over the years, Sandler clients in every major vertical have implemented—and benefited from—the principles covered in this book. The key to success is not only the content you will read here (although the content is vitally important). It's the ongoing reinforcement from Sandler.

Is the SES Process Only Relevant to Selling Teams That Target Very Large Organizations?

Most of the SES Tools are relevant to all sales teams. As for the program as a whole, it applies best to firms selling to decision makers within larger entities.

Our Selling Situation Is Unique. How Do I Know SES Is Right for Us?

The collaborative nature of SES allows it to fit well into any organization that sells into the enterprise space. The wide portfolio of tools that drive the program allows clients to focus on the specific tools that best map to their unique business models; those tools are customizable to fit the unique needs of a client's particular selling environment. If your team is responsible for enterprise selling, SES is right for you.

What's My Next Step If I Want To Learn More About SES?

Visit www.sandler.com/enterpriseselling or contact your local Sandler office.

Territory & Account Planning

Understand the process for developing business planning strategies to meet sales objectives in two key areas: territory planning and account planning.

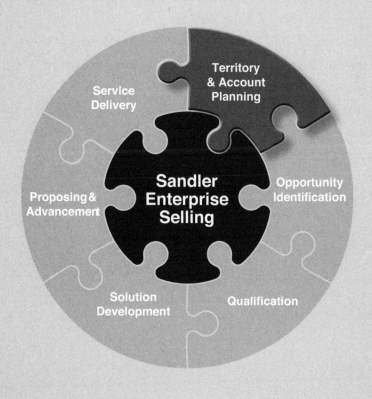

*A lot has to happen before you reach out
to a prospect or client about a specific
enterprise opportunity. The critical
first step, of course, is planning.*

In chapter 1, **Market Understanding**, you'll focus on how to get to know your market better than anyone.

In chapter 2, **Analysis/SWOT Assessment**, you'll develop an understanding of the best ways to do what you do best.

In chapter 3, **Client/Prospect Profile Development**, you'll categorize your enterprise opportunities using Sandler's proprietary KARE system.

In chapter 4, **Territory Value Propositions**, you'll determine the best way to highlight the value you bring to your territory when it's considered as a whole.

In chapter 5, **Account Planning**, you'll focus like a laser beam on account planning, using a proprietary Sandler tool called the Growth Account Booster.

CHAPTER 1

Market Understanding

Territory planning, the focus of chapters 1 through 4 is the process of collecting and analyzing appropriate data and the building of practical strategies based on that data to maximize the likelihood of success.

Effective territory planning is the bedrock upon which the successful achievement of personal and organizational enterprise selling goals is built. This kind of planning focuses broadly on accounts within a given territory and on the identification of the product or service with the value most relevant to them.

"Which are the most promising, most likely prospects for our organization's products and services?" Exploring this question closely and continually drives the best possible return on investment. Good enterprise territory plans are living tools. They are not documentation that sits in a binder on a shelf. They must be reviewed and amended moving forward, based on the dynamic conditions in the marketplace.

> ## SANDLER ENTERPRISE SELLING RULE
>
> *Know your market better than anyone.*

A True Story

A family-run regional office equipment distributor—let's call the company *Copy Top*—hired a new VP of sales. We'll call her *Jeri Lane*. Jeri was to replace one of the firm's three founding brothers, who was retiring.

Up to this point, the Copy Top sales force had not followed any formal account planning process. Brainstorming sessions were conducted annually for each account generating more than $200,000 in annual business. These sessions included sales management and all the members of the sales team, and the results were typically the same after each session: make more calls, do more cross-selling, target decision makers who are higher in the organization, and so on.

Jeri faced some challenges. In recent years, Copy Top's client-retention numbers had slipped, and accounts generating $200,000 in revenues were vanishing. These larger accounts had provided 75 percent of company revenues eight years before, but now provided only 52 percent. The trend line was ominous. Jeri rightly saw this as a huge issue and led an effort to inject active account planning for the 20 top-revenue-generating Copy Top clients.

After doing a little digging, Jeri found there was a profound lack of understanding about these critical clients' business objectives. Just as troubling, there was a pervasive disconnect between the sales and service teams. She brought the two teams together for a series of special account planning sessions and included people from other key functional areas of the firm, such as accounting and marketing.

These meetings helped to build an organizational understanding of the clients and their businesses and led to the development of a health-care-focused division to serve this particular vertical, which (Jeri pointed out) provided 46 percentof Copy Top's total revenues. The account planning discussions also included a key focus on Copy Top competitors and, through feedback from the service team, it was recognized that one competitor was relentlessly targeting Copy Top's large clients—and winning their business.

Jeri implemented a defensive strategy that focused on a new client satisfaction process. Within 12 months, the competitive challenge was thwarted. Jeri also convinced HR to amend the sales and service compensation structures to provide similarly designed bonuses for client retention and account growth. Within two years of her taking the job, client retention of Copy Top's 20 most important accounts stood at 95 percent—and overall revenues from accounts generating $200,000 or more now contributed 74 percent of the firm's revenues. Account planning had turned things around!

Know Your Surroundings

Some organizations execute the market planning piece really well. Others don't spend enough time on it and, as a result, take off without solid footing.

In the world of enterprise selling, you have to generate market understanding before you do anything else. It's not a "nice-to-have" asset. It's mandatory!

There are six key areas to build market understanding: account base, economy, service structure and deployment, market patterns, competition, and affiliations/alliances. While there may be others, these six are critical. The listing below breaks down the specific inquiry points connected to each area. How many of these bullet points sound familiar to you?

Account Base

- Likely vertical focus
- Typical company size
- Common pains
- Typical sales-cycle length
- Revenue potential
- Competitive positions
- Commercial vs. public sector

Economy

- Market cycles
- Seasonal buying patterns
- Regional influences
- Growth
- Vertical impacts
- Governmental issues
- Environmental issues

Service Structure and Deployment

- Direct/remote
- Internal/outsourced
- Product/service based
- Team selling focus
- Alliance/channel partners
- Industry specialization
- Practice/specialty groups
- Organizational support

Market Patterns

- Demographics
- Buying access
- Brand image
- Ethical issues
- Cultural issues

Competition

- Footprint
- Customer view/acceptance
- Growth pattern
- Sales/marketing strategy
- Pricing model
- Distribution methods
- Territory value propositions

Affiliations/Alliances

- Industry/trade associations
- Local colleges and universities
- Current clients from other territories

- Current channel partners
- Current alliance partners
- Current prime/sub-partners
- Chambers of commerce
- Company alumni/friends
- Other affiliations/alliances

During SES training, participants are asked to pinpoint all of the above, being as specific as possible, and then to identify the one topic with the biggest impact on their business in each of the six categories. Why not do it now before you move on to the next chapter?

CHAPTER 2

Analysis/SWOT Assessment

Proper analysis and assessment positions you to develop effective strategies that strengthen your competitive advantage and increase the likelihood of personal and organizational success. Spending quality time in this disciplined analysis process will provide focus and precision when it is time to evaluate prospective targets.

SANDLER ENTERPRISE SELLING RULE

Do what you do best.

What Is a SWOT Analysis?

A SWOT analysis, or SWOT matrix, is a structured planning process that evaluates strengths, weaknesses, opportunities, and threats relevant to a project or business venture.

Seller, Know Thyself!

Having established your market understanding as a foundation, you now move to developing a comprehensive understanding of your strengths, weaknesses, opportunities, and threats. As a result, you need to decide what you do well and what you do not do so well. You enhance that knowledge by assessing what external variables will likely affect you positively and negatively. This brings you to the next part of the SES process, which is all about determining what you do well and seeking the most favorable conditions in which to do it.

Teddy Roosevelt once said, "Do what you can, where you are, with what you have." He could have been offering advice about conducting and acting upon a good SWOT analysis.

Many companies have used the SWOT approach over the years; it's among the most popular executive planning tools. What's often forgotten is that the strengths and weaknesses look internally while the opportunities and threats look externally.

The SES version of this tool emphasizes this by placing *strengths* on the top and *weaknesses* on the bottom. Take a look at Figure 2.1 now. Notice the action verbs that illustrate strengths, weaknesses, opportunities, and threats.

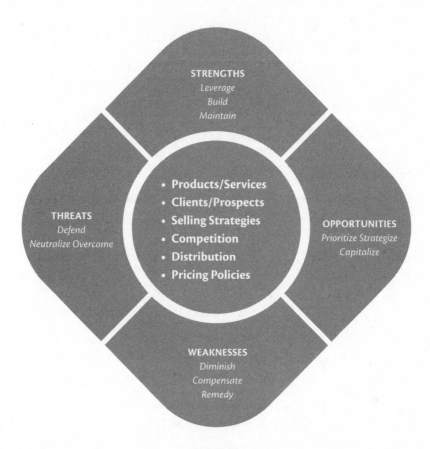

We want to leverage strengths, prioritize opportunities, diminish weaknesses, and defend against threats. The center highlights some elements that enterprise-selling organizations must classify as a starting point of this exercise. Thus, distribution may be a strength for some and a weakness for others, while competition may be either an opportunity or a threat.

Figure 2.2 is an example of a completed SWOT assessment for territory planning, which is an excellent place to start.

What can you determine from the items that this company has identified as S, W, O, and T? What do you think about this company's position? What actions could they take to improve their situation?

Build on your strengths, work on your weaknesses; exploit your opportunities, neutralize your threats. Why not complete this territory planning SWOT exercise for your own team, before moving on to chapter 3?

CHAPTER 3

Client/Prospect Profile Development

To develop meaningful profiles for clients and prospects, you can use Sandler's proprietary KARE Account Planning tool, which adds clarity to planning and decision making. It delivers tremendous value to all enterprise-selling teams. Figure 3.1 shows the four components of the tool.

Keep	**Attain**
Recapture	**Expand**

A Tough Question

What system are you using right now to categorize your enterprise prospects and clients? Do you use revenue? Vertical market designations? Geographical location? Company size?

Most of the teams Sandler trains have no formal system of categorization in place. When they are asked what system they use to categorize their enterprise prospects and clients, they sometimes try to camouflage their lack of a system by saying things such as, "Every account is unique."

Whenever people say, "We don't have an account categorization system because we treat each account as a unique relationship," the answer is, "That might sound good, but there's a problem. If every account is unique, you can't create a territory management plan. There has to be some overarching strategy, some kind of categorization, if you're going to manage the whole territory effectively."

What are some of the categories you might use to distinguish different accounts? Consider the following.

- Current clients you want to **keep**.
- Accounts you don't have, but wish you could **attain**.
- Customers you used to have and now would like to **recapture**.

- Current accounts where you wish your "wallet share" could **expand.**

Put it all together, and it spells KARE!

Keep, Attain, Recapture, Expand

KARE is a powerful profile-development tool that takes into account these differences. KARE profiling is an effective strategy component in territory management that tags each of your prospects and clients with a single designation: keep, attain, recapture, or expand.

There's a famous British saying: "Horses for courses." It means different people are suited for different situations. The same is true of our prospects and accounts. They're not all alike.

One to a Customer

The KARE acronym tags each of your prospects and clients with a simple designation. This should be done for each of your active or potential accounts. No account can be in two KARE categories—you will have to pick one.

KARE presents an invaluable opportunity to prioritize your accounts. It also provides clarity and a common vocabulary for account identification. This is a major advantage in enterprise team selling, where cross-organizational collaboration is essential to winning and serving business.

Figure 3.2 shows the most common attributes arising from a KARE profiling session. The actual attributes relevant to your market must arise from your own evaluation of your selling organization's business model.

Keep	Attain
Current maintenance client	New business target
Acceptable profitability	Profile match
Minimal growth potential	Low level of vulnerability
Low level of vulnerability	Projected acceptable profitability
Acceptable relationships	Projected acceptable growth potential
Minimal investment	Acceptable pursuit investment
Managed service costs	Neutral relationships

Recapture	Expand
Inactive previous client	Current major client
Low level of vulnerability	High profitability
Variable growth potential	Strong growth potential
Acceptable profitability	High level of vulnerability
Variable relationships	Significant relationships
Variable pursuit investment	Investment target for growth

NOTE: It's possible that you have a prospect who does not align with your business objectives or a current client you have concluded, for whatever reason, you do not want to continue serving. Your decision to end the relationship professionally represents an action that must be undertaken separately from the KARE process.

Again, the KARE attributes are helpful, but they're just a starting point. They need to be customized to the world of the clients with whom you're dealing. Customizing KARE to your world allows you to make the system your own. Once you do that, you can segment and prioritize based on your own criteria. That's how you create a shared base of understanding and inquiry in the team-selling environment. Fortunately, this is very easy to do. It's also an indispensable learning experience for the team.

The KARE tool provides an invaluable sales management benefit, playing an integral role in territory and portfolio management and planning.

One strategy might be to focus certain sales reps or teams on particular profiles, such as gearing hunters toward A (attain) accounts, and farmers toward E (expand) accounts. Or, the focus might be to blend into each team and/or territory a mix of all account profiles, in order to keep reps and teams nimble and capable of serving different account types. It all depends on your strategy. Without KARE, you're in the dark. It's like the famous duck test. If it waddles like a duck, swims like a duck, and quacks like a duck, it's likely a duck. But until you know that the waddling, swimming, and quacking are all attributes of a duck, you have no enabling information.

KARE is your prime asset when it comes to territory and account planning.

CHAPTER 4

Territory Value Propositions

After effectively developing deep market understanding and analyzing what has been learned via SWOT, you saw how the KARE process delivers critical information about specific clients and prospects. Now what?

It's time to connect the dots. Here, in step four, you will leverage your focused market knowledge to craft territory value propositions.

Connect the Dots

Territory value propositions connect the dots between what you do well and the accounts you target. These written statements are the basis for building value throughout the sales cycle: from the 30-second commercials, discussed in Stage Two, to the customized, opportunity-specific value propositions in Stage Four. Your work here will be integrated throughout the program.

Because of the quality research and planning you've done to this point, you know your target markets, your strengths, and the profiles of your clients and prospects. To bridge the gap, concisely communicating the pro forma value of what you will ultimately deliver to your targets is crucial.

Let's assume that you're working for a printing company and your planning has identified the legal services market as a primary focus area. Thanks to the territory and account planning work you did earlier, you know the typical pains and needs of an account in that space. You will soon be learning how to craft your specific account plans, but at this point you're simply focused on building powerful, confidence-inspiring propositions for that targeted vertical market in general.

The best value propositions are short, direct, and high-impact. They shouldn't take weeks to put together, nor should they take hours to explain. Other programs demand three-day off-site sessions to develop value propositions, but Sandler believes that they need to be practical and useable in the real world of selling. Sandler views effective value propositions as the product of a concise, easy-to-understand "value arrow" process.

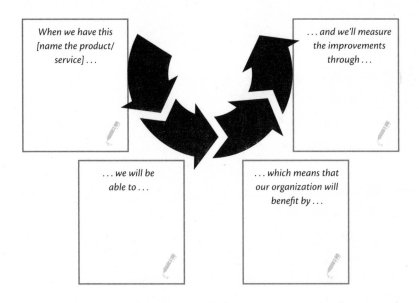

First, you name what the product/service is; then, you say what it does; next, you say how that benefits the client; and lastly, you say how that benefit is to be measured. How simple is that? That's the complete value proposition formula, stated in 30 seconds or less!

FOUR VALUE ARROWS

The value proposition should lay out clearly: what it is (i.e., what the product or service is called), what it does, how that delivers benefit, and how the benefit is measured.

Imagine being able to engage with a prospect and having a basic, verticalized understanding of what your product would be, what it would do, how it would benefit, and how the benefit would be measured. Actually, you don't have to imagine! Consider this global on-demand printing services firm's territory value proposition, developed for the international legal services market:

> "The Acme local printing capability allows us to print on-demand in 120 countries, meeting contract and project deadlines, and cutting printing costs by 74 percent."

Consider that the same printing company has chosen health-care providers as its other key vertical target market. Of course, the health care territory value proposition will be different than the one for the legal services market, as the vertical pains are unique to the industry.

Here's another example. This is an Internet marketing firm's territory value proposition, developed for the pharmaceutical market:

> "The Zilko web-based portal allows us to leverage the web to increase our speed to market and cut our product launch marketing costs in half."

These territory value propositions connect the dots. They offer a clear link between the value of the product or service and the relevant territory factors. They support a practical mindset that builds confidence in salespeople, who then create greater clarity in communication with prospects. Of course, much remains to be done (later in the program) to customize the territory value proposition to a specific opportunity, but what you've done here gets the ball rolling.

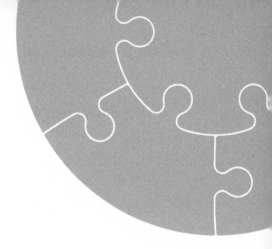

CHAPTER 5

Account Planning

Your efforts up to this point have helped ensure that you are focusing on the right prospects. Now, with the candidate accounts identified, you must build plans for each individual target. This is account planning.

<table>
<tr><td>SANDLER ENTERPRISE SELLING RULE</td></tr>
<tr><td>Hunt in packs.</td></tr>
</table>

Enterprise Roadmaps

Account planning in SES utilizes Sandler's proprietary Growth Account Booster tool to create detailed roadmaps for each account.

These account-level roadmaps involve discovery, mapping, goal-setting, and execution—all designed to win, maintain, and grow specific enterprise clients. Your goal now, whether you are dealing with a brand new account to attain, an account you want to recapture, or a current keep or expand client, is to maximize your delivery of value for the account as well as the extraction of value for your firm. To achieve these goals, you must not only create but also regularly update roadmaps for each account—roadmaps based on high-quality, nimble, client-focused account planning. These are practical plans, not academic white papers. They are dynamic real-time tools that drive advances and forward motion to help you win business.

The Teamwork Factor

How important is teamwork in an enterprise-selling environment? It's essential. Without teamwork on the selling side, nothing good happens for long. Good salespeople in the enterprise world know that people love to engage, and they encourage that engagement internally. They also know that there is a unique need for effective planning collaboration across the various internal silos of enterprise team selling.

The Growth Account Booster session had been designed to meet that need. As the first example of high-level internal selling-side collaboration, it's a planning event that takes team selling to a new level.

CHECK YOUR SECRECY AT THE DOOR

Collaborative planning in the enterprise world requires full, prompt transparency about all the developments that affect or could affect an account. This may mean that some members of the enterprise team need support in unlearning old habits of withholding information from colleagues who work in other areas of the company until the last possible minute (or later).

Enterprise organizations are very complex and diverse; so it is critical to develop team selling strategies that continuously earn and re-earn the right to serve, obtain, and expand significant accounts. That's what the Growth Account Booster tool does. It drives collaborative development of a targeted growth plan involving multiple players.

This tool is always focused on one specific enterprise account and follows a comprehensive 10-step process.

1. **The introduction.** This is where you get an overview of the tool and the purpose of the session.
2. **The establishment of the relevant sales team information.** Here, you decide who's doing what on the sales team.
3. **The relationship snapshot of the account.** This is where you detail critical past history, current data, and competitive information.
4. **The client cast of characters.** In this step, you look at who's who in the target account. It covers traits,

tendencies, and action items needed to enhance the relationships.

5. **The five-year account revenue span.** This looks backward and forward in terms of revenue generated and/or to be generated from the account.

6. **Current sales activity.** What have you sold recently and what is in the pipeline? The answer is here.

7. **Account relevance.** Here, you get specific in terms of how deep and wide you've gone in the account up until now, and how effectively you've delivered the breadth of the offerings in your product/service portfolio.

8. **The current top six opportunity pipeline.** This gives you a look at the most significant opportunities within the target account.

9. **The top six client value propositions.** Here, you create specific value propositions for each of the six opportunities. Do you remember the value arrows process you used for the value proposition? That's critical here.

10. **The top six opportunity advancement actions.** This gets specific about the forward motion you anticipate. What team actions will you take to grow the account?

The RACI Accountability System

The successful Growth Account Booster session is driven by accountability. It utilizes the well-known RACI process for assigning responsibility levels to all participants. The sales lead assigns one of the following responsibility tags to each participant in the Growth Account Booster session and clarifies each participant's role.

R = Responsible. These are the people who do the actual work necessary to get the job done.

A = Accountable. This is the one person who is ultimately accountable for the completion of the task and who delegates to those responsible.

C= Consulted. These are the people whose counsel is sought and with whom communication flows in both directions during an initiative.

I = Informed. These people are simply kept in the loop on the initiative's progress. Typically, communication with them is only in one direction, but they're free to weigh in at any time.

The Life Blood of Your Business

The Growth Account Booster session is a critical component of your enterprise selling campaign. It focuses on account growth, which is the life blood of your business. This is a hard-hitting, high-impact, present-tense planning tool that brings the internal team together. It's not a documentation-oriented tool. It takes territory planning to the account level. It's a comprehensive team exercise, requiring cooperation, specific time commitment, and full buy-in.

Get your hands on a Growth Account Booster tool (Figure 5.1)—identify your most important account—then schedule this team meeting!

Growth Account Booster Tool

Client: *Cool Heat Apparel*

Sales Lead: *Jen Adams — Sales Lead*

Date: *July 11, 2014*

AGENDA
• Introduction
• Sales Team Information
• Relationship Snapshot
• Client Cast of Characters
• 5-Year Account Revenue Span
• Current Sales Activity
• Account Relevance
• Current "Top 6" Opportunity Pipeline
• Client Value Propositions
• "Top 6" Opportunity Advancement Actions

Introduction

As the complexity of organizations has become wider and more diverse, sales organizations must develop team selling strategies to effectively earn the right to serve and expand significant customers. The Growth Account Booster process provides a well-planned account planning, growth and expansion tool that drives collaborative development involving the sales, operational, and delivery teams involved in pursuing key prospects and enterprise clients. Also involved may be representation from other functional areas in the selling organization that are connected, in some relevant way, to the specific prospect/client. Included may be representatives from Finance, Accounting, Legal, Market as well as practice groups, service lines and other connected organizational entities. Growth Account Booster incorporates all four key steps in the Account Planning process – Account Profiling, Decision Network Analysis, Targeted Opportunity Focus and Action Strategy. The tool is populated with as much information as possible by the prospect/client's sales lead prior to the Growth Account Booster session. The session's participants clarify and add to the information, collaboratively driving to action items as a team. And this tool will utilize a process for assigning responsibility levels to all of the participants involved to provide clarity of roles. This process, called RACI, which you will also see utilized throughout the Enterprise program, assigns one of the following responsibility tags to each participant in Growth Account Booster:

    R = Responsible – The people who do the actual work to get the job done.

    A = Accountable – The one person who is ultimately accountable for the completion of the task and who delegates to those Responsible.

    C = Consulted – The people whose counsel is sought and with whom communication flows in both directions during an initiative.

    I = Informed – Those simply kept in the loop on progress and with whom the communication is typically only in one direction.

And the process may be executed to varying levels of detail depending on the size and importance of the prospect/client organization involved. While Growth Account Booster is most effectively conducted as an in-person workshop, remote attendance, GoToMeeting and conference call formats often present more realistic alternatives. Taking the time to build goal-oriented and time-bound growth plans with a key focus on accountability is a critical component of team selling, customer satisfaction and account success.

To learn more about Sandler's proprietary Growth Account Booster tool and other key tools we've mentioned in this part of the book, visit www.sandler.com/enterpriseselling or contact your local Sandler office.

STAGE 2

Opportunity Identification

Identify and nurture opportunities in enterprise accounts.

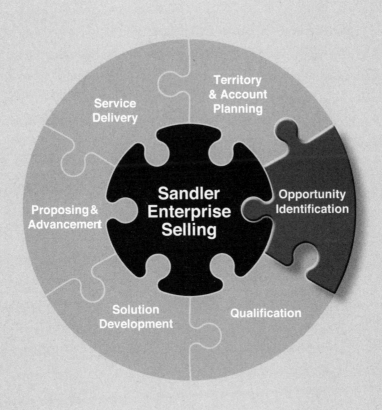

> *Stage Two builds on all of the work you did in Stage One. Territory and account planning now logically evolve to the opportunity-development level.*

In chapter 6, **Prospecting**, you'll focus on structured enterprise prospecting activities, covering the basic Sandler principles that support effective enterprise opportunity development.

In chapter 7, **Engaging**, you'll learn how to research and connect with enterprise prospects using social media. Specifically, you'll learn how to use Sandler's proprietary LinkedIn Levers Tool.

In chapter 8, **Communication**, you'll look at building relationships through targeting your messages effectively to your target market. You'll develop an understanding of the traits and tendencies of a diverse network of buyers. And, you'll learn how to use Sandler's proprietary Relationship Builder tool.

In chapter 9, **Setting Expectations**, you'll discover the importance of setting mutual expectations in every transaction to maintain control and to ensure forward motion. You'll find out how to create deeper understanding on all sides with every interaction, so you can keep everything on track. And, you'll learn how to use an important tool for setting and meeting stakeholder expectations internally: Sandler's proprietary Three Opportunity Planner tool, which focuses salespeople on opportunities that can be won in the short term, regardless of size.

CHAPTER 6

Prospecting

There is no one answer to the question, "What's the right enterprise prospecting formula?" It's a combination of prospecting activities that will be determined by customized factors in your world and your business model. But one thing is certain. In the enterprise world, as in all other professional selling, prospecting is about consistent, daily action. David Sandler said, "You don't have to like prospecting, you just have to do it." This is just as true in the enterprise world as it is anywhere else. You have to feed the funnel constantly.

SANDLER ENTERPRISE SELLING RULE

Feed the funnel.

The Keys to Prospecting Success

Prospecting and selling effectively require the mastery of three components. You have to learn and understand the role **behavior** plays in your performance; you have to learn the importance of and gain some control over **attitude**; and you have to learn and understand the importance of **technique**. In addition to all of that, goals and goal-setting are extremely important.

Most people think of success in terms of accomplishments, such as winning a major account, reaching sales goals, winning sales awards, or getting promoted. All of these achievements are signs of success and are the result of the convergence of those three core elements: behavior—goals and action plans with daily accountabilities; attitude—outlook and expectations; and technique—strategies and tactics. These are the three points of the Sandler Success Triangle as shown in Figure 6.1.

Most sales-training courses focus on only one of the three elements: technique. Salespeople learn the latest techniques for cold calling or closing a sale. Once the training is over, they might even try to implement them. The results, however, are short-lived—not because the techniques didn't have merit, but because they didn't fit with the salesperson's behavior or with the salesperson's perception of what he or she could achieve.

Technique training without behavior and attitude training may increase your short-term sales, but technique training alone will not take you to the top.

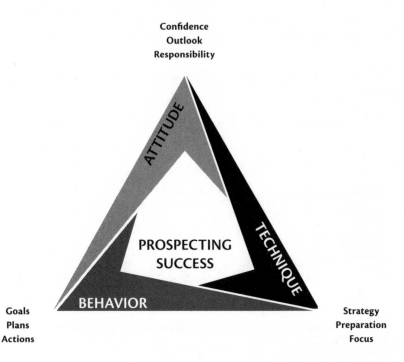

The problem is that the technique, or "mechanical," side to selling is relatively easy to learn but much more difficult to put into practice. Why? Because selling is mostly conceptual, not technical or mechanical. Conceptually, you have to be comfortable incorporating the techniques into your own personality.

All three corners of the Success Triangle are vitally important. They must be constantly reviewed, revisited, and reinforced over time.

What's Your "BAT"-ting Average?

Here's a quick summary of the three points on the Sandler Success Triangle.

- **Behavior:** daily, habitual accountabilities, "muscle memory"
- **Attitude**: accountability for your feelings about your life
- **Technique:** accountability for what you do and say

The most important point of the triangle to work on varies by individual. However, most salespeople don't have a problem identifying good techniques.

Develop an Enterprise Prospecting Plan

With an understanding of the work you completed in Stage One: Territory & Account Planning and an understanding of the importance of behavior, attitude, and technique, you can focus on building a prospecting plan that is customized to you, your company, and your target market. You have many powerful tools from which to choose.

Remember as you move forward that the key is to execute the plan you develop. Be sure to include benchmarks and methods that will allow you to adjust the plan along the way. Most of all, be sure to prospect consistently according to your plan. To develop that plan, begin by asking yourself:

- How many contacts, conversations and touch points do I need to have in a given month?
- From what sources will those contacts and conversations come?
- How many from each source do I need each month?

Exercise: Prospecting Activity Goals

Use Table 6.1 to identify the relevant prospecting activities and targets in your world.

Week: _____

Activity/Preparation	Goal	Actual
Telephone prospecting calls		
LinkedIn, e-mail, or other interactive media		
Referral meetings		
Networking events		
Total Contacts		

Use the chart as a first step. Set up a measurable enterprise prospecting plan for yourself and for the team—and then start implementing it!

THE LAST WORD ON PROSPECTING

"Every unsuccessful sales call earns compound interest."

–David Sandler

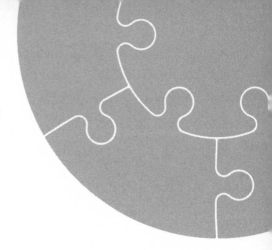

CHAPTER 7

Engaging

I n the SES program, participants are trained to develop an enterprise-focused, territory-specific 30-second commercial. This commercial builds on all the work you did in Stage One, and naturally follows the territory value propositions you created there. As the value/pain connection is integrated throughout the SES program, the 30-second commercial will grow more and more targeted. Right now, you're developing a commercial for the territory as a whole.

SANDLER ENTERPRISE SELLING RULE

Use the first impression to create value.

Let's go back to the territory value propositions you crafted when you were evaluating the market needs.

Remember the four value arrows:

1. "When we have this [name the product/service] . . .
2. ". . . we will be able to . . ."
3. ". . . which means that our organization will benefit by . . ."
4. ". . . and we'll measure the improvements through . . ."

Before you take a close look at what follows in this chapter, you will want to reacquaint yourself with your work on these four points. All of that work is likely to connect to your first pass on the development of a powerful enterprise selling resource: your territory-driven 30-second commercial.

Harness the Power of Your First Impression

You can't stop people from making a quick decision about you, but you can act in a positive and targeted way that gives you an early advantage. That's exactly what the 30-second commercial is designed to do.

Any effective 30-second commercial, and certainly this territory-focused one, must be short and direct. Remember: when you deliver this commercial, you are not selling anything at all. The commercial generates interest and is the catalyst for a good conversation in any number of settings, including a prospecting call.

The commercial should cause the other person to wonder:

- "How do they do that?"
- "How would that work in my situation?"
- "How much would this cost?"

Be prepared to spend a significant amount of time developing the pain indicator statement. It must be customized to your product/service and to the territory you are serving. The 30-second commercial is the heart of your stress-free prospecting call—and the heart of your 30-second commercial is its pain indicator statement. (You'll be learning much more about the Sandler concept of "pain" in Stage Three.)

Some Sample Pain Statements

Here are some examples of effective pain statements.

- **For an advertising specialties firm:** Our clients recognize that quality products, competitive prices, glowing testimonials, and industry awards don't mean a thing if your potential customers don't remember who you are or how to get in touch with you.
- **For a marketing consulting firm:** Typically, our clients are financial firms who came to us because they were tired of spending a lot of money on glitzy advertising campaigns that were unique and memorable, but didn't bring customers through the doors.
- **For a law firm:** We work with clients who are concerned that they aren't receiving the value they expected from their current attorney. Or they are feeling frustrated because they are using two or three different small specialty firms to handle their matters, which is costing them more. Or they are upset that the attorneys from different firms don't coordinate their efforts to come up with a business-wide strategy for the company.

Take a moment now to develop a pain indicator statement that would resonate for the typical prospect within your territory. Ask yourself:

- Why do your clients buy the type of product or service you sell? What problems do you help them solve or avoid? What goals do you help them achieve? What pain do you alleviate?
- Why, specifically, do they buy from you rather than someone else? What do you have to offer that they can't obtain from your competitors?
- What would your clients give up by not buying your product or service or by not buying it from you?

What Goes Before and After?

Once you have an effective pain indicator statement, it's time to create the rest of the commercial. Typically, there is an introduction, a capsule summary of the business that includes the pain indicator statement, and a hook question.

Table 7.1 is an example of how it might all come together. Notice that the discussion is "scripted" only in the sense that it has a 30-second commercial that culminates in a hook question. Beyond that, it is simply a conversation between peers.

Introduction		Your name, company name and type of business (if not evident by the name). Example: *This is Terry Simms with Transcom International Freight.*
Capsule Summary of Your Business	**Pain Statement**	The specific pain(s) which your product/service address(es). Example: *We provide international freight forwarding services for your counterparts at large companies who frequently need expedited service and are frustrated about delays and missed deadlines that cause problems for their clients.*
	Benefit Statement	Solution that your product/service provides. This should be based on the value proposition(s) you created in Stage One: Territory & Account Planning. Example: *Because we own our containers and have exclusive leases with both air and sea carriers, we can accommodate expedited shipments that have dramatically better on-time performance than what most companies are accustomed to receiving.*
Hook Question		Question to determine whether your product/service is relevant to the prospect. Example: *I was wondering...how often do you need expedited overseas shipments?* or *What benefit might there be to offering your overseas customers expedited deliveries, if you didn't have to worry about late shipments?*

Table 7.2 shows how this would look during a prospecting phone call.

ELEMENTS	EXAMPLE
Opening	• Introduce yourself (name and company). • *Did I catch you at a particularly bad time?* • *Do you have two minutes to speak on the phone and determine whether or not you and I need to have a conversation today?* • If the prospect says "yes" to the first question or "no" to the second, say: *When would be a better time to call back when you would have two minutes to talk?*
Up-Front Contract	• *Would it be OK if I briefly tell you why I've called and then you can decide if we should continue the conversation? Are you comfortable with that?* • *Suppose I briefly explain why I've called and then you tell me if we have something to discuss. Would that make sense?*
30-Second Commercial	• Insert the pain statement, benefit statement, and hook question from your 30-second commercial.
Close	• *Based on what you're telling me, it sounds like it would make sense for you to invite me in to discuss this further. What do you think?* • *May I make a suggestion? Why don't you pick a day when you can invite me over to discuss this further?*
Post-Sell	• *Can you think of anything that will come up between now and then that would force you to cancel the appointment?*

A key point about using the outline above is in order here. Once you pose the hook question, you must stop talking and wait for the other person to respond. Avoid the temptation to fill the "awkward" silence. Let the other person do that. Then do whatever is necessary to support a peer-to-peer discussion about the presence or absence of pain you can alleviate.

This kind of call is far more effective than a traditional prospecting call, which is more of a steamroller than a conversation. Because Sandler's stress-free prospecting call imposes less pressure on each side, it creates a safe place for a professional conversation—a conversation that leads to a clear, mutually beneficial next step that both sides can agree on ahead of time.

At this point, you may be wondering how to handle the questions that the other person is likely to raise during this call and the roadblocks that arise during the initial conversation. This will be covered in chapter 8, Communication. For now, just focus on developing and practicing your 30-second commercial and integrating it into the calling structure that's just been outlined.

LinkedIn Levers

As this book goes to press, LinkedIn has some 400 million members in over 200 countries and territories. More than 120 million are from the United States. It's the world's largest professional network. You simply can't ignore it. Why would you want to?

When it comes to the most valuable information required for research in individual enterprise clients and accounts, LinkedIn is the best source available. It's the gold standard, and reviewing it closely should be considered a mandatory requirement for all enterprise pursuits.

You can rest assured that the sophisticated competition you face in the enterprise arena is all over LinkedIn. Not only that, it's highly likely that your prospects and clients are using it to research you and your company as well. LinkedIn is not a "nice-to-have," but a "must-have!"

Let's take a look at Sandler's proprietary LinkedIn Levers Tool. Figure 7.1 is a sample, with all the right information in the right spots.

Notice that this is a two-tiered checklist. This example is researching a primary individual contact along with the target company as a whole.

Some people overlook LinkedIn corporate pages during this research step. That's a mistake. While corporate websites have value, LinkedIn corporate pages have deep substance. For example, the Under Armour corporate website is very well done, but consider what someone at Sandler's home office got from researching their corporate LinkedIn page. In one area alone, he saw that of the 5,000 Under Armour employees with accounts on LinkedIn, he was connected in the first or second degree to 500 of them. What a database! That is real substance that you can convert to meaningful action on a pursuit.

By the way, if you move into the realm of paid LinkedIn subscriptions, and specifically the Sales Navigator application (which is excellent), you can leverage the first- and second-degree contacts of everyone in your organization.

This tool provides a simple way to get the most critical research information in a concise, quick manner. It takes research up a notch and provides the substance you need to build competitive advantage. The best thing is that most of this information can be found very quickly and easily on LinkedIn. Think about the value you gain as a selling organization from all that you are learning. Think about the

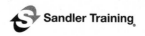

LinkedIn® Levers Tool

Use this checklist for ideas to consider when using LinkedIn to research specific contacts and their company.

Researching the client:	*Tom Donovan*
Do you have any mutual connections with the client?	*Yes, 4 first connections and 23 second.*
How many connections does the client have?	*500+*
Which college attended and degree attained?	*Loyola University, BA, MIS.*
What is the client's hometown and current city?	*Originally from Wilmington, NC, and now living in Towson, MD.*
Where did the client work previously?	*Turner Consulting, GT Strategies*
How much time did the client spend at previous jobs?	*4 years at Cool Hot, 5 years at GT and 7 years at Turner.*
Which companies and groups does the client follow?	*Loyola Univ. Alumni, ISOM, Turner Alumni, GT Strategies, TGT, EMC, KOL Apparel*
What type of info does the client post/share? Which influencers does he follow?	*Not a frequent poster*
What activities and interests does the client list?	*None noted*
To which industry groups does the client belong?	*National Retail Association, E-Comm Network, Paymetric, Data Storage Professionals*
Does the client endorse others? Is he endorsed often and for what?	*BI – 86, E-Comm – 51, Strategy – 34, ERP – 22, Vendor Management –19*
Has the client been recommended by anyone? If so, by whom?	*10 personal recommendations by supervisors and co-workers.*
Does the client support any charities or initiatives?	*Habitat for Homeless*
Researching the company:	*Cool Hot Apparel*
How does the company present itself in its profile? Are there any key themes?	*Leading edge in technology, highest quality, "every product makes you better."*
What competitors are identified in the company's "also viewed" section?	*KOL Apparel, Land Sports, Scoreboard Fits, Leopard, Old Balance*
Do you have any connections with former employees?	*497 first or second connections.*
Is the company currently hiring full-time employees? In what areas?	*Yes, in many areas – product management, marketing, business analysis, editing, etc.*
What key products/services does the company highlight in its profile?	*"CH Life" theme features CH people, "Be humble, stay hungry."*
Can you identify any connections after scrolling through the company's employee list?	*Yes, at least 6.*

opportunities you now have to connect via shared contacts, alumni organizations, LinkedIn groups, and other channels.

The populated tool offers a fictional example of how this might work. In this case, Tom Donovan's work history, shared first- and second-degree connections with him, and the identification of six shared contacts with the company's employee list are examples of critical information that is easy to find using LinkedIn.

A *True Story*

Natalie, a sales rep with Des-Eye-Near Services, an interior design firm in Nashville, Tennessee, had obtained an RFP from LifeFitCare, a local health care system with three hospitals and twenty clinics in the greater Nashville area. She had mobilized her proposal team, and they had devoted three weeks and significant money to preparing the response, which was due in one week.

In assembling the pursuit team for a strategy session, Zach, representing Des-Eye-Near's finance group, asked Natalie who from LifeFitCare would be making the actual decision. Natalie shared that Ned Thompson, LifeFitCare's COO, was the primary decision maker.

Curious, Zach checked Ned out on LinkedIn and discovered that he followed only three groups. One was UT Martin Alumni, which made sense, as Ned was an alumnus. The second group was the Nashville Business Executive Networking Roundtable. Nothing surprising there. The third group, however, was Nashville Design Dynamics, Des-Eye-Near's biggest competitor!

Based on Zach's discovery, Natalie made a call to Ned and discussed his affinity to NDD. Ned indicated that he was "open to all prospective vendors" and that Des-Eye-Near would get a "fair shake," but confirmed that he had been working with NDD for over a decade and was quite happy with the relationship.

Translation: NDD had the inside track and was unlikely to lose it. Natalie reported the details of the call to the pursuit team, and the decision was made to end the pursuit and redeploy the team members on other initiatives. Needless to say, discovering that critical nugget of information earlier in the process would have saved Des-Eye-Near lots of time and money. It was an expensive way to learn a simple lesson: check LinkedIn!

Engage Effectively

Use LinkedIn and other online portals to support face-to-face and voice-to-voice interaction with prospects. Don't imagine you can do everything digitally. You can't. The more you engage with clients face-to-face or voice-to-voice, the clearer things become and the easier it is to determine what you should be doing next.

The LinkedIn Levers tool brings you into alignment with the reality that much of our initial engagement with enterprise contacts is going to begin online with LinkedIn. There is no replacement for face-to-face and voice-to-voice communication, of course, but by the same token, there is no denying that, in today's business world, LinkedIn is and will likely remain an essential resource in any effective initial engagement strategy.

There's a lot more to learn about LinkedIn! For a copy of our article "10 Ways to Use LinkedIn to Prospect More Effectively," visit www.sandler.com/news-and-media/free-sales-training-material.

CHAPTER 8

Communication

Once you've engaged with a prospect, it's important to make sure your communication is effective—often easier said than done. Take a look at Figure 8.1, which breaks down how human beings communicate.

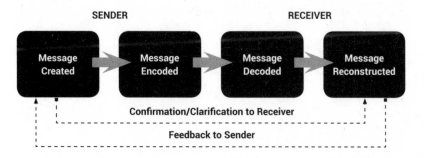

What could be simpler? Yet even though this communication model seems quite direct, things often get deeply confused when you are interacting with stakeholders and decision makers. Why?

The answer is straightforward: People have different behavioral profiles. What works with one person may backfire spectacularly with someone else.

This brings us to the DISC behavioral assessment system, which is deeply relevant to the world of sales and to the world of enterprise sales in particular. Sellers in this environment must interact and build alliances with people who present broadly differing behavioral styles.

SANDLER ENTERPRISE SELLING RULE

*People buy from people they like and
from people like themselves.*

Exercise: Buyers and Sellers— The Four Behavior Profiles

This exercise will help you master interpersonal communication in the enterprise world—and everywhere else. Consider the following categories, associating each of the four profiles with people you know. (You'll get the most out of this exercise if you follow the directions given.)

- **PROFILE 1:** "I have high standards. I work systematically. I'm precise. I find out the facts. I'm cautious, careful, and conscientious. I'm rigorously analytical. It's extremely important to me to be accurate and well-organized. My secret fear is being forced to choose between quality and relationships because I will lean toward quality."

On a separate sheet of paper, jot down the name of a colleague who fits this description. Then jot down the name of a prospect or client who fits this description. Do it right now, before you read Profile 2.

- **PROFILE 2:** "I'm a self-starter and a born risk-taker. I love solving problems. People say I have a healthy ego. I am direct in my dealings. I live to make decisions. My secret fear is that someone will take advantage of me."

On a separate sheet of paper, jot down the name of a colleague who fits this description. Then write down the name of a prospect or client who fits this description. Do it right now, before you read Profile 3.

- **PROFILE 3:** "I'm extremely enthusiastic, talkative, and persuasive. I draw energy from groups and thrive in social situations. I motivate others to achieve at a high level. I am usually optimistic. People sometimes say I'm too emotional. At my best, I'm downright inspirational. My secret fear is rejection."

On a separate sheet of paper, jot down the name of a colleague who fits this description. Then write down the name of a prospect or client who fits this description. Do it right now, before you read Profile 4.

- **PROFILE 4:** "I'm a great listener, loyal to the end, and eager to understand you. Some people call me 'the ultimate team player.' Relationships mean a lot to me, and I don't like to let an ally down. I'm a peace-keeper. I'm reliable and dependable. My biggest fear is a loss of security."

  On a separate sheet of paper, jot down the name of a colleague who fits this description. Then jot down the name of a prospect or client who fits this description. Do it now!

Finally, choose the profile that most closely describes you. Write that on your sheet, as well. Please don't continue reading until you've written everything down.

The Four DISC Behavior Profiles

- People aligned with Behavioral Profile 1 are likely COMPLIANTS.
- People aligned with Behavioral Profile 2 are likely DOMINANTS.
- People aligned with Behavioral Profile 3 are likely INFLUENCERS.
- People aligned with Behavioral Profile 4 are likely STEADY RELATORS.

DISC is a behavioral model that is used to categorize the way people interact with one another. It takes its name from the initials of the four participatory styles it uses. These styles are usually listed in the following sequence, so that they're

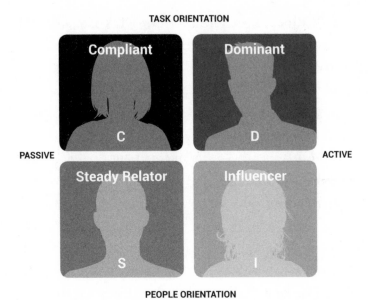

easy to remember: Dominant, Influencer, Steady Relator, and Compliant. (See Figure 8.2.) Let's look at each of the profiles in depth.

Behavior Profile: Dominant

Dominants are extroverted, often opinionated people who need to take action. They like to be in charge of situations. When they aren't in control, they are uncomfortable. They are bored if they aren't challenged. Dominants do not like small talk. They like to win and get ahead. They are not natural team players, but they do tend to be organized (in their own way), direct, and to the point, all of which can make them valuable members of the team. With high D's, you need to tell them the bottom line, give them a few choices, and then let them decide how to proceed. Make the ground rules and tasks clear from the very start. Present these logically, and make a clear up-front contract. If high D's are part of developing a solution, they will be more satisfied. High D's are at their best when they can reach their own conclusions. Be prepared to listen as high D's are always eager to share their opinions and ideas. Because high D's like to be in charge, they are not easy to manage. If they are called on for team selling, they may need extra coaching. Since they are action-oriented and opinionated, they need to learn to listen and to work at the slower pace of others. Dominants can be emotional and may need to learn to manage their expressiveness with both clients and colleagues.

Behavior Profile: Influencer

Influencers are personable and trusting. They like to talk/interact and leave the action to others. Since they want to be liked, they are eager team players. Influencers are creative and humorous, but they also tend to strike others as disorganized. They can be impulsive and intuitive, relying on feelings, and they are not logical decision makers. Influencers require a friendly, sociable approach in which they are not rushed or controlled. They like to combine business with pleasure; they don't get "down" to business, but get "around" to business. They are very sensitive to public criticism and disapproval. They like talking in terms of ideas, feelings, and people—not facts and figures. Their optimism might lead them to presume, rather than plan, for successful outcomes. They lack the discipline for follow-up work. High I's who work as salespeople, for instance, may trust prospects to follow through, overlooking post-selling the terms of a deal or payment. They set high performance goals, but may not plan the details of attaining them. They need to learn to ask questions such as: "How exactly will you do that?" and "What exactly are the terms for delivery of this job?" Coaching can help high I's use facts and figures in their presentations, complete detail work, and manage their emotional impulsiveness when dealing with clients and colleagues.

Behavior Profile: Steady Relator

Steady Relators are amiable, patient people who know how to keep the peace and avoid conflict. Since they practice and prefer constancy and consistency, they don't like changes or surprises. They are deliberate and can appear slow to make decisions. High S's are loyal, with long-term commitments. They don't reveal their true feelings often. Taking a sincere interest in their personal goals and concerns can win you their loyalty. They dislike interruptions when at work on a task, as well as hard-sell tactics or being rushed to a decision. Since high S's are unsettled by change, they need plenty of time to anticipate new procedures, changes in job responsibilities, or shifts in company structure. High S's are not complainers, but their natural peacekeeping tendencies prevent them from being completely honest. They shrink from disagreements, but can benefit by having problem-solving procedures set up ahead of time. Deal with conflicts directly, but give the high S's plenty of space to deal with differences. Voicemail, e-mail, or memos give high S's time to digest and respond. Remember that high S's tend to give others the same type of leeway they require. Being pressed for a firm commitment can sometimes feel dangerous to them. Work in stages and respect the high S's relationships. The high S needs a steady pace.

Behavior Profile: Compliant

Compliants are cautious thinkers. Detail-oriented perfectionists, their high standards follow the book. Since they are busy getting one more fact in search of the perfect answer, they may be slow, or even unwilling, to commit to a course of action. High C's are analytical and orderly in their thinking and acting, relying totally on facts and figures. Forget small talk and pleasantries. Get to the point and give high C's the facts presented in an organized, logical fashion. Give them time to look at every angle and consider all options before requesting a decision. High C's often find initial discussions with new contacts to be particularly challenging. Their lack of people orientation makes creating rapport difficult. They may overlook another person's needs and concerns and may tend to overwhelm people with data. As perfectionists, they are very sensitive to criticism and the recurrent risk of rejection inherent in sales. If you are a high D or I, your relationship with high C's is likely to be difficult. High I's are exactly the opposite of high C's, and building trust with the high C will likely be difficult for the high I. If you are a high D, there is good news and bad news when it comes to the high C. The good news is that you are also analytical and task-driven, so there is likely to be some common ground. The bad news is that the high C's demand for more detail and more time to reach conclusions will seem particularly frustrating.

Consider the relationships between the four profiles as shown in Figure 8.3.

C – Compliants

C-STYLE:
- Use data and facts
- Examine an argument from all sides
- Keep on task; don't socialize
- Disagree with the facts, not the person
- Focus on quality
- Avoid new solutions; stick to proven ideas
- Do not touch
- Allow time to think

Dominants – D

D-STYLE:
- Be direct, brief, and to the point
- Focus on the task; stick to business
- Use a results-oriented approach
- Identify opportunities/ challenges
- Provide win/win situations
- Use a logical approach
- Touch on high points; do not overuse data
- Do not touch; keep your distance

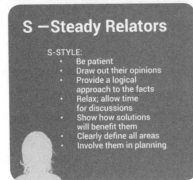

S –Steady Relators

S-STYLE:
- Be patient
- Draw out their opinions
- Provide a logical approach to the facts
- Relax; allow time for discussions
- Show how solutions will benefit them
- Clearly define all areas
- Involve them in planning

Influencers – I

I-STYLE:
- Allow time for socialization
- Lighten up; have fun
- Ask for feelings and opinions
- Create a friendly, non-threatening environment
- Involve them in brainstorming new ideas and approaches
- Expect quick decisions
- Provide opportunities for recognition and reward

A True Story

Eric, a high I, worked for a company we'll call *QNE Data Solutions*. Eric was a very successful salesperson who sold high-end services to enterprise buyers in the IT world. He had a high level of confidence and experience, and he had a reputation for creating relationships easily and quickly within the buyer network. Year after year, he posted great numbers. His great skill was creating superb relationships with individual buyers, typically high I's, like himself, or high D's.

Then something changed. When the economy started to tighten up, Eric found himself in a different position. The buyers who typically had bought his services on their own authority and on the strength of their trust that Eric would keep his word (which he always did) now started telling him that other people were involved.

In the aftermath of the financial crisis, a new approach to buying had taken hold in Eric's market as different departments were consolidating their purchases. Eric found himself dealing more and more with the corporate buyer. Suddenly, he realized that he wasn't making the sales that he used to make. Now, instead of those high I's and high D's he was used to connecting with, and connected with easily, he was in front of high C's, too. These buyers were analytical. They looked for process. They could and did kill deals where the process was not crystal clear.

Because of the intangible nature of his company's service, Eric had, up to that point, focused on selling future benefits. He was selling things that were going to happen in the future, based on his own commitments and his ability to fulfill them. Historically, those high I and high D buyers had responded quite well to that. Now the game had changed. The new buyers wanted step-by-step breakdowns of exactly where they were now, exactly where they were going, exactly what was going to happen next, exactly what resources were needed, and exactly how long it was all going to take. Not only that, they wanted documentation and proof: proof of what was going to happen in each of the steps and proof of ROI. None of this came intuitively to Eric.

Eric's market had changed dramatically. These were the same companies, and he was selling the same service. All of his old high I and high D contacts were still in the loop. But they were accompanied by new high C contacts. Eventually Eric realized why he wasn't selling nearly as much to those client bases. Things only turned around when he invested time and attention in learning the DISC system and mastering the new "language" of his high C buyers.

No Villains, No Heroes

A behavior profile is neither right nor wrong. It's just how people operate.

Developing rapport with a prospect is an integral part of the selling process. It is the salesperson's responsibility to create a comfortable environment that facilitates communication and helps build mutual trust and respect—not just at the beginning of a discussion, but throughout the selling process. If you create that kind of mutual trust and respect, you will have a significant competitive edge for yourself and your organization.

Sometimes people imagine they are doing a better job of this than they actually are. That's because it's easy to ignore or minimize the importance of identifying a contact's behavioral profile. Treating the entire world as though it were populated by people who share, or should adopt, your behavioral profile cuts you off from 75 percent of the people with whom you could be engaging. If you are a professional salesperson, and certainly if you are a professional salesperson operating in the enterprise environment, you have an obligation to learn how to speak the languages of the groups that don't overlap with your own behavioral profile. Studying Figure 8.3 is a good place to start.

The Wake-Up Call

Consider the following simple "wake-up call" exercise for enterprise salespeople.

Think of your number one opportunity in a specific enterprise account. Now, how many people within that account could you reach out to over the weekend and expect to hear back from before Monday morning?

The response from most SES training participants is "zero." Not only that, but typically the cast of characters that the sales team knows within that account is only one or two people. That's not a great way to enhance the odds of winning an enterprise pursuit.

Participants are then asked: "So, if that's your number one opportunity, you know only one or two people there and none of them are close enough to you to return your call on a weekend, what does that say about the rest of your opportunities?" It's a good question, isn't it?

Salespeople sometimes make the mistake of thinking that the quality of the engagement is more robust than it actually is. That's where Sandler's proprietary Relationship Builder tool comes in handy.

The Relationship Builder Tool

The Relationship Builder tool provides a simple baseline to chart all of an account's key decision makers—the cast of characters. It identifies information on each individual's personal goals and the perceived wins that connect to those goals, along with descriptive data on each contact's traits and specific relationship with the selling firm. Most importantly, this tool outlines action plans for each individual and specifies next steps to enhance the key relationships. The emphasis on action is a common thread in the SES program. It always focuses on forward progress. It encourages individual client action plans that are based on steps you can take to enhance the value of the relationship.

Here's a question for you: In a perfect world, based on the accounts you've sold in the past, what kinds of people do you want to have on your radar screen? Ideally, you'd want to have relationships with all the different possible stakeholders in an account who have actually played a major role in past buying decisions. By definition, since you're selling in the enterprise world, that's going to be more than "one or two people." Some key players may not even be on the formal organization chart—there could be a former executive, for instance, who is called in to consult on major decisions that connect to your product or service.

IMPROVE THE CONNECTION

The Relationship Builder tool helps to deepen connections with key players.

As noted earlier, salespeople can be an over-optimistic breed. The classifications in this tool call for brutal honesty and specific plans, so the action items can be credible and well-targeted.

The Relationship Builder tool (Figure 8.4) helps you create action plans crafted to enhance each individual relationship.

For each person, you have to create specific action items or value enhancers, both for the short term and for the longer term.

By the way, if crafting these kinds of action plans is difficult for you, that means you still have some research to do on the opportunity.

Relationship Builder Tool

Account:	WSD Global Port Services	KARE Designation:			Keep

Cast of Characters

Client Contact	Role	Personal Goals/Wins	LinkedIn Connected? (Y/N)	DISC Style D, I, S or C	Existing Relationship (Friend, Neutral, Enemy) F, N or E
Nirav Patel	Chief Marketing Officer	WSD Americas Presidency	Y	D	N
Alexa Timmons	Marketing VP	CMO	Y	I	F
Peter Sikorsky	Marketing Director	Integrated System	Y	C	F
Elena Sebescen	Marketing Analyst	?	N	?	?

Individual Client Action Plan

Contact:	Nirav Patel	Alexa Timmons	Peter Sikorsky	Elena Sebescen
Value Enhancers: (Three actions you can take now to enhance your relationship)	Deliver effectively on BPK Project	Deliver effectively on BPK Project	Deliver effectively on BPK Project	Deliver effectively on BPK Project
	Introduce Nirav to NYU Board	Deliver effectively on "T-Time" Project	Deliver effectively on "T-Time" Project	Set meeting with Elena to build relationship
	Invite Nirav to join Client Advisory Panel	Accompany Alexa to Client Summit	Promote Pete's blog to FGM network	Provide Elena access to LMS
Value-Enhancer Outlook: (Three actions you can plan for in the long-term future to enhance your relationship)	Complete BPK Project	Complete BPK Project	Complete BPK Project	Complete BPK Project
	Meet annual performance goals	Close "T-Time" and win Phase II	Close "T-Time" and win Phase II	TBD
	Provide speaking platform at annual summit	Introduce to NY Metro Women's Leadership Council	Provide speaking engagement at Regional User Forum	TBD

CHAPTER 9

Setting Expectations

This chapter is all about establishing the ground rules. What are ground rules, and what do they have to do with enterprise selling or any kind of selling? Think of what happens before a baseball game or a boxing match. The umpires or the referee meet with both sides. There's an important discussion that happens before the first pitch is tossed or the first punch is thrown. The purpose of that preliminary discussion is to review what's in bounds, what's out of bounds, what special rules apply, how the winner of the contest will be determined, and how special situations will be handled. Everyone agrees about the ground rules before things get started in earnest.

Something similar happens when a professional salesperson begins a discussion with an enterprise contact. The sales professional sets the ground rules by means of an Up-Front Contract.

The phrase *up-front contract* refers to the Sandler process for maintaining control of the conversation, adding predictability to the selling process, making sure that you and your prospect are on the same page, and playing by the same rules. The ground rules always include the specific objectives for the discussion.

There are major disadvantages to not having an up-front agreement with the prospect about the ground rules. Without an up-front contract, you have no agreement about the process by which objectives will be reached, no real engagement with the other person, and no shared understanding of what both sides are doing. Clear agreements become less likely, and that means a win/win outcome becomes much less likely.

SANDLER ENTERPRISE SELLING RULE

Agreements drive actions.

Five Components of an Up-Front Contract

Following are the five components of a good up-front contract.

1. **Objective.** There should be a clear objective for each contact with a prospect—one that moves the selling process forward.
2. **Time Considerations.** The scheduled duration of the call is just as important as the time and date of the call but is often overlooked or downplayed. If your call is going to take two hours, for instance, the prospect must agree to invest that amount of time.
3. **Prospect's Agenda.** If you expect your prospect to be prepared to discuss particular matters or provide certain information, he must know that before the

discussion starts and agree in advance to do so. Otherwise, in relation to your expectations, the prospect will be ill-prepared for the meeting.

4. **Salesperson's Agenda.** You must let your prospect know your intended actions for the meeting, and the prospect must be okay with them.

5. **Outcome.** Each encounter should have a defined ending—a decision to be made (perhaps a choice to move the discussion to the next level by involving others in a scheduled meeting) or some other conclusion to be reached (maybe to continue one-on-one discussions or end the process). The outcome should be specifically defined and agreed to in advance. "Playing it by ear" is not a good strategy. Neither is "wishing and hoping" that something good will happen.

Don't feel handcuffed by this list. There are hundreds of different ways to hit all five of those requirements as you begin a discussion with an enterprise prospect.

More Than Just a Selling Tool

A question that is posed in the SES program is: Are conversations with prospects the only time to discuss the ground rules, set expectations, and make agreements?

Of course, the answer is "no." The up-front contract is vitally important when members of the selling organization are interacting with each other. They are vitally important in discussions between the selling and delivery teams and between management and individual salespeople.

Clear agreements about ground rules and clear expectations are just as essential internally. Specifically, clear mutual agreements must be part of the conversation when it comes to forecasting business. With that in mind, let's look at the next SES tool, which is all about setting and meeting practical expectations internally.

The Three Opportunity Planner

While enterprise pursuits are typically characterized by long sales cycles and significant financial investments, the accounts routinely offer smaller opportunities as well. These accounts are transaction engines. Streams of business opportunities over time typify enterprise relationships. The larger deals, of course, are critical and deserving of focus—but so, too, are the smaller opportunities. They generate revenues, satisfy clients, open new doors, and lead to expansion opportunities after they've been won. These smaller deals can connect you to new opportunities, constituencies, and allies. It's like the old saying: "Mighty oaks from little acorns grow."

SHOW ME THE MONEY

Sooner and smaller is more accurate for income/cash-flow predictions than later, bigger and less certain.

Here's the point. As an enterprise seller, you aren't just interested in what will close. From a planning standpoint, you have to be interested in the answer to, "What can I close quickly?" These are typically smaller deals.

The Three Opportunity Planner tool provides a clear focus on the three highest-probability opportunities that are likely to close soon—typically within the next 60 calendar days. That 60-day standard is a good starting point, but it isn't written in stone. Use whatever short-term time frame makes sense for the Three Opportunity Plan, based on your business model; however, the best planning often turns out to be approximately 60 calendar days.

Two important principles emerge here. First, there must be some agreed-upon short-term time horizon between manager and salesperson. Second, forecasts against that horizon must be based on reality, not wishful thinking. Without clear agreements between selling professionals and the managers who coach them based on these two principles, we're likely to hear dangerous exchanges like this:

Manager: So what's in your pipeline, Marco?

Salesperson: Oh, I'm working on a big deal. A very big deal.

Manager: Great! I love big deals. Which one is this?

Salesperson: HugeCo. You were in on that meeting, remember?

Manager: Oh, yes, I remember that. What's the projected value on that?

Salesperson: Two hundred gazillion dollars.

Manager: Great. When's it projected to close?

Salesperson: Well, it's got a lot of moving parts. It's going to take a while. Let's say two years from now. Leave me alone until then and let me do my job, okay? I'm really busy with this opportunity. It's quite complex.

Manager: Okay, no problem. Just keep me posted.

The problem is, while HugeCo may technically be an active prospect (in the sense that the discussions are moving forward and some mutually agreed-upon next step is in place), you still need a backup plan. Suppose something goes wrong with the HugeCo deal? Suppose you learn that a competitor is entrenched there? Suppose the decision cycle is not two years but three years? Suppose its likelihood of closing is actually only 5 percent?

That's the pattern to avoid: salespeople putting all or most of their selling time into the HugeCo deal. Too often, that's exactly what enterprise sales teams do. Why are salespeople sometimes tempted to focus on bigger deals as the only priority, instead of smaller ones that will close more quickly? Big deals mean big dollars, and there are social rewards for being part of a team that closes a big deal. Winning a big deal carries with it the possibility of long-term potential for both the individual and the organization. For these reasons and any number of others, it's easy to get distracted by the potential of big wins. So you have to set up plans that compensate for that tendency.

SMALL IS BEAUTIFUL

Larger and longer-term deals are critical to your territory's overall portfolio, especially in the enterprise world—but you still need to pay the bills while those major pursuits unfold over time. That means frequent wins. And these have to be planned ahead of time.

Closing deals of any size earns you the right to turn a prospect into a client. You do that by exposing new stakeholders within the enterprise to the power of your solution as it plays out in the real world. Small victories are the easiest, fastest way to do that.

So let's take a close look at this next tool, the Three Opportunity Planner tool as shown in Figure 9.1. It is designed to help focus on the need for frequent wins of any size.

Three Opportunity Planner Tool (TOP)

Sales Lead: _____

| Three Highest-Probability Deals Closing within 60 Days | | | | | |
Account	KARE	Opportunity	Value	Probability	Close Date
1.					
2.					
3.					

| Three TOP Deals: Value Propositions | | |
Account	Opportunity	Value Proposition
1.		
2.		
3.		

The tool's collaborative sharing of the planned actions with relevant members of the selling organization maximizes the likelihood of winning. Notice that the KARE account designation process and the RACI accountability system each figure prominently here.

Agreements, Contracts, and Shared Expectations

How important are up-front contracts and shared expectations in the world of enterprise selling? If you want to generate mutually beneficial outcomes for your team and your clients on a consistent basis, these contracts are about as important as oxygen.

Clear discussions about ground rules and about shared, real-world expectations are what make success possible. They are not only essential to interactions with your prospects, but also to your interactions with team members within the selling organization. Agreements really do drive action.

Once you're clear on that point and on the rest of the opportunity identification process, it's time to move on to the third stage of the SES program: qualification.

A Sandler trainer can help you make developing good up-front contracts and using the Three Opportunity Planner a way of life. To find a Sandler trainer in your area, visit www.sandler.com.

STAGE 3

Qualification

Develop an understanding of the qualification process
in selling and serving enterprise organizations.

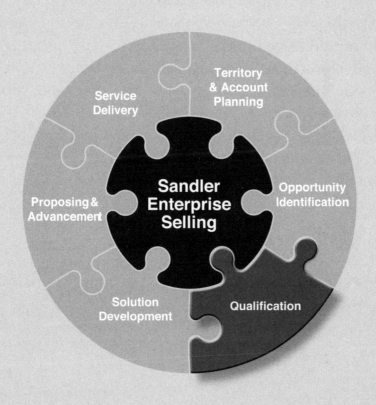

> *This stage is the core Sandler concept*
> *of qualification—not everyone deserves*
> *your time and resources. Your job in*
> *Stage Three is to find out who does.*

In chapter 10, **Positioning**, you'll gain an understanding of how your competitors on an opportunity are likely to present their value to the prospect.

In chapter 11, **Teaming**, you'll explore the collaboration that occurs on both sides of the pursuit.

In chapter 12, **Pain—Establishing Reasons to Do Business**, you'll launch the qualification process in earnest by getting clarity not only on what enterprise prospects want, but why they want it.

In chapter 13, **Budget**, you'll continue the qualification process by identifying the buying organization's willingness to invest in a solution that resolves all of the pains.

In chapter 14, **Decision**, you enter the final part of the qualification process by uncovering all the relevant information about the enterprise decision-making process.

CHAPTER 10

Positioning

H ere in the qualification stage, you are focused on making credible, strategic business decisions about pursuing specific opportunities. Everything you do here drives action items and next steps—the forward movement of SES.

Four Qualification Tools

There are four proprietary Sandler tools you will be using in this stage to move specific opportunities forward: the **Positioning Tool,** the **Pre-call Planner Tool,** the **Call Debrief Tool,** and the **Opportunity Tool.** All are based on fundamental Sandler principles, as applied to the enterprise world.

What has happened up to this point? You have done territory and account planning to increase the likelihood that the business you pursue is the business you're most likely to win. You've followed structured prospecting activities, engaging and communicating with prospects, and setting the right mutual expectations. Now, at the level of the actual opportunity, you drill down further. Let's begin with the process called "positioning."

> ## SANDLER ENTERPRISE SELLING RULE
>
> *Know your competitors so well that*
> *they bring out the best in you.*

The Big Question

What would you say is the single most important thing for you to understand about your competition?

You'd be surprised at the wide range of answers participants give in SES training sessions. People say the most important thing to understand about a competitor on an enterprise pursuit is anything from their strategy, their product/service, the markets they serve, to their pricing.

Actually, Sandler says the most important thing to understand about the competition in the enterprise world is their value proposition for a specific buyer in a specific opportunity.

If you know how the competition is positioning themselves for the business you want, then you can position your own offer more effectively. That's the answer to the big question. If you could wave a magic wand and learn one thing about what your competitors are up to, that's probably what you'd want to know. Why? Because your own value proposition should outflank the competition's. If it doesn't, you'd want to know that in short order.

At this point, it's a good idea to review the four-part SES definition of a value proposition as shown in Figure 10.1. Look at the value arrows once again.

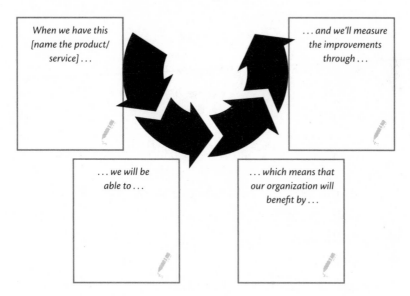

When we have this [name the product/ service] . . .

. . . and we'll measure the improvements through . . .

. . . we will be able to . . .

. . . which means that our organization will benefit by . . .

There is nothing wrong with studying the competition's history and offerings, but success in the enterprise world requires that you develop an understanding of the value propositions your competition will likely bring to the opportunity you are pursuing.

At this point, it's not uncommon for salespeople to tell us, "I have no idea what the competition's value propositions are." Sandler's proprietary Positioning tool helps you get a little closer to figuring that out. Let's look at it now.

The Positioning Tool

The Positioning tool provides a clear, simple template for identifying the customized value of your product or service as compared to the competitive options available to the enterprise account being pursued.

> *"Know your enemies and know yourself."*
>
> —Sun Tzu

Positioning your product or service properly often requires in-depth analysis and research. The Positioning tool begins that research process, gives you a clear picture of the likely cast of characters, and helps you create a competitively aware action plan.

In Figure 10.2, you see a portion of the Positioning tool. To prepare for a positioning session, you should:

- Consider a significant opportunity you are currently pursuing, then identify each key buyer within that opportunity and rate your relationship with each of them. Is this person a friend, neutral, or an enemy? Also make your own best identification of each person's impact on this deal (high, medium, or low), and DISC style.
- State the solution you plan to present in terms of the four elements of the value proposition.

- Identify the key competitors. What are their strengths? What are their weaknesses? Who are their coaches? What presence do they currently have within the account? What value have they delivered in the past? What next steps will you take to identify the competition's likely current value proposition? (For instance, what internal allies could you ask about this? When will you do this?)

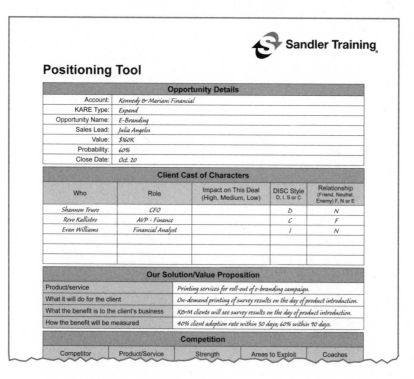

CHAPTER 11

Teaming

Considering the work discussed thus far, you probably grasp the basic importance of team selling. Now it's time to focus on this aspect of the enterprise sale in depth because you can't expect to qualify the opportunity without a team approach.

One of the reasons team selling is particularly critical in the enterprise world is that enterprise organizations buy in teams. Since buying organizations bring functions from across the enterprise to the buying center, selling organizations need to use team selling to fortify their initiative and to be able to face off, functionally, with buyers. Everyone on the selling team must be aware of the importance of qualification and must be willing to support the goal of effectively qualifying the prospect.

> *"If you're not serving a client, then serve someone who is."*
>
> —Jan Carlzon, *Moments of Truth*

The Team and the Plan

Most sales teams do not create a written plan for an upcoming meeting with a prospect. During SES training programs, participants are asked: How many people have ever gone into a meeting or a call with a prospect without doing any written planning whatsoever? All the hands go up. Next question: How many people here have ever lost a sale—and then seriously wished they'd done some planning? Again, everyone's hand goes up.

Why is planning not always second nature to salespeople? A lot of it, it turns out, has to do with the fact that some salespeople—and even some entire teams—may think of written planning as a means of control dreamed up by some authority figure or another. They hear the word *planning* and they think, "Uh-oh—sounds like paperwork. And paperwork sounds like the opposite of freedom!"

In the world of enterprise selling, discipline equals freedom. Once you assume personal and team accountability for a little discipline, specifically for planning and sharing your plan with your colleagues better than the competition does, you realize you can have all the autonomy and freedom that success brings. Sales meetings are too important to "wing it"!

With that in mind, it's time to look at an extremely simple tool that can help everyone on the selling team make planning easier, more effective, more shareable, and, yes, even more enjoyable.

The Pre-call Planner

Sandler's proprietary Pre-call Planner Tool helps you set up the plan for a meeting with enterprise buyers. (See Figure 11.1.) It encourages solid collaboration and good information-sharing on the selling side. This tool is based on the principle that buyers are people too.

Too often, buyers are typecast by sellers as hard-nosed and narrowly focused. Enterprise buyers are typically more well-rounded than that and should be treated as the sophisticated business people they are. Each must be approached as an individual. The importance of considering the DISC styles of specific buyers, in particular, cannot be overstated. If the prospect's main buyer turns out to be a high-D, bottom-line oriented, "get-to-the-point" person and the primary contact on the selling side is a high-C, process-driven, "connect-all-the-dots" type, the situation may call for a team that includes someone who is as bottom-line oriented as the main buyer. Similarly, a situation that points to a long selling cycle calls for a team that also includes someone with the stability and patience necessary to see a long, complex cycle through to the end.

Notice how much essential ground this simple tool covers in a small amount of real estate and how simple it is to complete before the meeting.

Pre-call Planner Tool

Sandler Training

Selling Team Attendees:	Jenny Archer, Sr. Sales Representative		Chris Teller, Business Development Manager		
Account: Tempest, Inc.		Date of call: Nov. 5, 2014		KARE Designation: Expand	

Cast of Characters

Client Contact	Role	Impact on This Deal (High, Medium, Low)	Met Before? (Y/N)	LinkedIn Connected? (Y/N)	DISC Style D, I, S or C	Existing Relationship (Friend, Neutral, Enemy) F, N or E
Lou Harper	VP, Sales	High	N	N	D	N
Maggie O'Toole	Sales Director	Medium	Y	Y	I	F

Selling Side: Have you prebriefed?

Relationship issues: Yes. Building relationship with Lou is critical.
Business issues: Yes. Potential acquisition of Tech-Draw Pharmaceuticals is key.
Roles/responsibilities: Yes. Chris to map to Lou at executive level.

What should you bring?

- Support materials Y
- Technical support NA
- Demo capability e-files NA

- Delivery/service examples Y
- Reference materials Y
- Other RSA Testimonial

Goals for call:
- Chris & Lou relationship start
- Tech-Draw update

- Commitment for Q2 business
- Next Year Outlook

Key questions to ask:
- How to prepare for Tech-Draw
- How we have met Client Satisfaction goals

- How Lou would like to be served
- How we can more effectively serve

Questions the buyer may ask you:
- What are you doing to prepare for Q2?
- Can you discount your pricing?

Your responses to these questions:
- What have you done in Pharma space?
- Can you customize our program?

Planned Up-Front Contract: Thanks & confirm time. Cover agenda — we'll ask about Q2, Tech-Draw, etc. and ask about customization, Pharma, etc. Confirm it's OK to say "no" and clearly outline next steps.

This is an extremely easy-to-use tool that increases the likelihood of success on an upcoming sales call by providing an organized team planning framework—a simple set of steps that allow you to maximize the potential of your next discussion with an active prospect.

A good lawyer wouldn't argue a case without preparing. A competent pilot would prepare before beginning a cross-country flight. Similarly, professional preparation is essential for successful client interactions.

The Pre-call Planner Tool helps you to identify key research items that connect to the people with whom you'll be interacting. It also helps you to design the specific up-front contracts and focused questions you'll be using during the discussion.

There are always two teams: the buyers and the sellers. Very often, the buying team has the upper hand. The Pre-call Planner Tool is a powerful resource for selling teams that levels the playing field.

The Call Debrief Tool

What does your sales team do right after that meeting you've planned so carefully? The answer's not that hard. You need another tool to debrief on what just happened.

If you have a formal, written debrief process for your discussions with enterprise prospects, you are much less likely to lose track of important details. Not only that, everybody on the selling side can catch up with what happened during the meeting. You now have an easy-to-circulate digital record of the meeting, which means you are likely to do better planning and be better prepared for your next discussion with that prospect.

Many salespeople resist using a formal debrief process. A lot of this has to do with the need for independence. But here again, there's a paradox at work: the better you debrief after a call, the greater your likelihood of success. The higher your level of success, the more personal independence you can claim.

Every single meeting with an enterprise prospect carries important lessons learned. If you don't quickly record those lessons after the discussion and share them with the other people in your organization, then someone on your side may forget them, or worse, never learn them at all. That would be giving up a huge competitive advantage.

Debriefing right after the meeting has to be a major priority in any enterprise pursuit. Fortunately, you have access to a quick and effective way to do a simple, formal debrief. It's Sandler's proprietary Call Debrief tool (Figure 11.2.).

This tool helps you discover the most valuable lessons learned from a sales call that has already occurred. It guides you through a solid debrief of the key takeaways, helps you detail any new plans that emerged, and encourages recording exactly what you uncovered during that discussion. This completed document is a major advantage for the team.

Think about it. How big an advantage is it to use this tool to capture all the major lessons you received from your key contact, right after the meeting? Huge! The sooner you capture the lessons learned, the more information you'll retain. Too often, the selling team decides to rely on memory when it comes to debriefing sessions. This is a major mistake. Write it all down!

Call Debrief Tool

Client Contact: *Ronnie Chang*

Client Organization: *Meister Financial Services*

KARE Profile: *Attain*

Selling team attendees:

* *Matt Daly — Sr. Sales Representative*
* *Jennifer Battles — District Sales Manager*

New information learned:

* *Meister is looking to make a significant acquisition by year-end to expand its West Coast presence.*
* *Ronnie is being considered for a promotion and a potential move to Chicago.*

Next steps planned:

* *Research the three potential acquisition targets Ronnie shared with us.*
* *Proactively propose pilot of development of Wealth Management Unit — present on Aug. 18.*

Red flags/potential problems uncovered:

* *There were concerns with our services on the Amisco Project — Tom Daniels to follow up on Aug. 19.*
* *Budget cutbacks and layoffs are possible for Q4 — Follow-up meeting with Ronnie on Aug. 22.*

Questions/topics for next contact:

* *Wealth Management study — as above.*
* *Due diligence results regarding Amisco Project.*

Action Steps:	Who?	When?	Intended Result?
Amisco Due Diligence	*T. Daniels*	*Aug. 19*	*Clarity on service quality*
Wealth Management Pilot Proposal	*M. Daly*	*Aug. 18*	*Gain client approval*

CHAPTER 12

Pain—Establishing Reasons to Do Business

I n the enterprise selling world, learning how to qualify a personal and organizational pain is vitally important. This is one of the skills that distinguishes sales professionals from amateurs.

<table>
<tr><td>SANDER ENTERPRISE SELLING RULE</td></tr>
<tr><td>No pain, no sale!</td></tr>
</table>

The stakes are very high here. Identifying pain is critical to the Sandler qualifying process, and the risks associated with not qualifying effectively are multiplied exponentially at the enterprise level.

Think about it. What happens if you misdiagnose pain at this level? You may waste time, money, and attention pursuing an opportunity that isn't a good fit or doesn't exist. You may walk away from an opportunity that is perfect for you because you didn't diagnose properly. You may lose out because you failed to pursue another opportunity entirely. None of those outcomes is what you want.

> ### WHAT IS PAIN?
>
> *Pain exists when there is a real or perceived gap between an existing situation and the desire for a better situation.*

The Pain Gap

Figure 12.1 is a diagram illustrating the Pain Gap. Pain exists when there is a real or perceived gap between an existing situation and the desire for a better situation. The selling team's solution must bridge the gap.

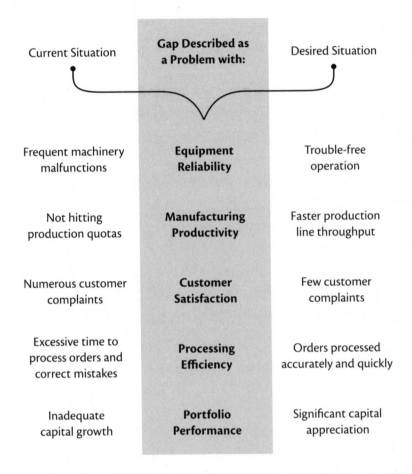

Current Situation	Gap Described as a Problem with:	Desired Situation
Frequent machinery malfunctions	**Equipment Reliability**	Trouble-free operation
Not hitting production quotas	**Manufacturing Productivity**	Faster production line throughput
Numerous customer complaints	**Customer Satisfaction**	Few customer complaints
Excessive time to process orders and correct mistakes	**Processing Efficiency**	Orders processed accurately and quickly
Inadequate capital growth	**Portfolio Performance**	Significant capital appreciation

Three pieces of information are required for a complete picture of pain—the problem, the underlying reasons, and the impact. Your job is to put together the pieces of the puzzle so you can identify a current prospect's problems.

Notice that the emphasis here is on the prospect's problems. Sometimes you get stuck thinking about your product/ service or its features/benefits. You can't stop there. After all, it's not about you! It's more important to look much more closely, at the specific problems and pains involved.

In Search of Big Problems

Think of your most important contact at your most important client. What is the single biggest problem you solve for that person and that organization?

If you can't express that in a single sentence, or if the sentence is built around features or product specifications, you've still got some work to do. Refine your answer to that question until it reflects the problem you solve—the pain you remove from the client's world.

The bigger the pain you can identify, and remove, the better your position within any given account. There is no way to win big revenue without identifying big problems.

Sandler Pain Funnel Questions

To get a sense of the dimensions and impact of the gap between where prospects are and where they want to be, you can use a questioning process known as the Sandler Pain Funnel (Figure 12.2). Notice that the questions in the funnel move from identifying the problem from the prospect's point of view toward a description of the ultimate impact if nothing is done.

Pain Questions

Tell me more about that . . .

Can you be more specific? Give me an example.

How long has that been a problem?

What have you tried to do about that?

And did it work?

How much do you think that has cost you?

How do you feel about that?

Have you given up trying to deal with the problem?

People are willing to take action to resolve a problem situation only when they fully realize the depth of their pain. Your organized questioning must take a prospect to that point.

The Opportunity Tool

Sandler's proprietary Opportunity tool (Figure 12.3) gives you up-to-date snapshots of three critical aspects of an emerging deal—the competitors involved, the client's key pains, and the action-oriented next steps most likely to generate positive outcomes.

With this tool, you can identify the biggest business problems that directly affect the client and the key actions that will take this business relationship to the next level. Once you do that, you're in a much better position to win the business. Without that information, you're competitively vulnerable.

Sandler Training

Opportunity Tool

Opportunity Details	
Account:	Devlin Mobility
KARE Type:	Expand
Sales Lead:	Debbie Murphy
Opportunity:	Sales Training

Competitive Landscape			
Competitor	Product/Service	Our Edge	Coaches (theirs)
Thomas Training	Sales Training	Legacy of Performance with sister company	Roger Downs – Sales VP
We-Sell On-Line, Inc.	E-Sales Training	Legacy of Performance with sister company	Jessica Harty – Purchasing Analyst

Client Pain Identification			
Pain Discovered	Business Implication	Identified Budget	Organizational Importance (aware, concern, critical, other)
Long Sales Cycles	High Cost of Sale	Average cost of sale - $28K/opportunity	Critical
Decreasing Hit Rate	High Cost of Sale, Sales Turnover	Above and Avg. Salesperson Hire - $230K	Critical
Client Retention	Revenue & Profit Loss, Sales Turnover	Three $500K+ Clients lost last year	Critical

For most selling teams, completing this tool is an ongoing effort. You start with all the competitors you know. If you know your competition and what they bring to the table, you should also be able to state the competitive advantage you have over them. Ideally, you should also know who their sponsors—also known as "coaches"—are within the account. You continue by identifying the key pains and the action steps that will have the biggest positive impact on this business relationship and sustain forward momentum.

By the way, not being able to come up with any portion of this information means you are looking at a red flag—a warning sign. There is more work to do to before you can proceed in this pursuit with credibility.

At the end of the day, selling is all about solving problems, and enterprise selling is about solving big problems. Once you identify the biggest problems and you can connect them to workable solutions from your side, you've got a real opportunity. On the other hand, if you're still missing information, if you found some areas where you still have work to do, that's good. That means you know what to do next. If you've got all the pieces of the puzzle in place and you know what your action steps are, take action! That's what SES is all about.

Internal Coaches

Your team needs a consistent flow of timely, accurate information about the organizations you are serving or seeking to serve, specifically the problems that need solving. Coaches are the people who help you get this information and guide you through the organizational maze. They're your internal advocates within the target organization, and you will need more than one.

Finding these internal point people may be as simple as asking your current contact for help. Try something like: Sean, it would really be great if I had someone to guide me through all the ins and outs of how your company operates. Would you be willing to help? You earn the right to ask that question by being the type of person other people are willing to help. As we all know, people buy from people they like.

You should have multiple coaches in every enterprise account on which you are calling, and the number depends on the size of the buyer network. These coaches should represent as many different functional areas of the firm as can be possibly penetrated.

- You want coaches from the **user group**: the group that ultimately interacts with your products/services.
- You also need coaches from the **buying group,** such as people in procurement, purchasing, supply chain.
- You should have coaches from the **technical group**: the team involved in making the decision due to its technical expertise.
- You also need multiple **influencer** coaches:. the people who are going to be affected by whatever you are selling but may not play a direct role in the buying process.

The people in these four groups all contribute to the way your offering is treated by the ultimate decision maker.

Influencers can be very helpful coaches in obtaining information for you. Because they have nothing to win or lose, they are less likely to filter or skew information. Influencers carry a lot of clout with key constituencies, including end users and economic buyers, and they can ignite an internal revolution toward, or away from, your product or service.

The ideal coach is the person with the greatest authority. Yet even if you are intimately connected to a decision maker operating at the top level, your offering must still be enhanced by information gained from coaches throughout the buying structure. Sometimes, the highest levels of an organization can be the last and least informed. This is why you must maintain information channels throughout the organization as you qualify for pain.

CHAPTER 13

Budget

B udget is a key element of the qualification process. Qualifying for budget helps uncover the prospect organization's expectations or limitations regarding the cost, price, or fees associated with the solution. Obviously, nailing down this information is immensely important in the enterprise world, especially when the investments in a pursuit are significant.

Willing? Able?

Is there a difference between *willing* and *able* when it comes to budget issues? Yes—a big difference, especially in the enterprise world. Some contacts are willing to work with you but are unable to move the budget discussion forward.

Willing minus *able* equals unqualified for budget. In order to justify continuing the pursuit, you have to broaden your discussion and engage other people.

In order for you to proceed, a prospect must be willing and able to invest:

- Money
- Time
- Resources
- Political capital

The Two Big Roadblocks

Let's also consider the situation where a contact may be 100 percent able to move the budget conversation forward, but is not yet 100 percent willing. There are two major categories of roadblocks likely to derail a discussion of the budget with an enterprise prospect: technical and conceptual.

Technical roadblocks are doubts about whether your offering will fit or work in this enterprise prospect's environment. Conceptual roadblocks are doubts about whether what you are offering fits into the organization's larger strategy.

You Get What You Ask For

Many people's comfort level when it comes to asking questions regarding budgets or discussing finance in general can be associated with their early childhood impressions about money.

Are you comfortable asking enterprise contacts direct questions about money? Why or why not?

Participants in the SES training program use the two columns in Table 13.1 to pinpoint all the relevant responses to that question. This helps them understand the messages they received about money as a child.

PLENTY	SCARCITY
There's plenty of money to go around.	Money doesn't grow on trees.
There's more where that came from.	I'm not made of money.
You have to spend money to make money.	Save your pennies for a rainy day.
You can't take it with you.	Don't discuss money matters with strangers.

Where were most of your responses: on the plenty side or on the scarcity side? Based on what you just learned about yourself, consider the following questions.

- Which of the childhood messages you heard about money had the biggest impact on you?
- Do your money messages help or hinder your selling efforts? How?
- Can you be too comfortable discussing money issues? What are the potential ramifications?
- What new attitude and behavior regarding money would better serve you in your sales efforts?

"Because that's where the money is."

—Willie Sutton, when someone asked him why he robbed banks

What Do I Say?

Sometimes people have challenges when it comes to figuring out the exact words to say when they ask about budget. Here's a list that can help. Of the following questions, can you pick out one that you are willing to pose verbatim during your next meeting with an appropriate enterprise contact?

- Is funding currently available? If it isn't, when will it be?
- What part does the price play in the final buying decision?
- Will the lowest bidder be chosen?
- Are there any limitations on the expenditure?
- How will the size of previous purchases for the same or similar products/services influence the amount invested for the current purchase?

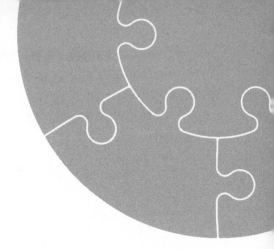

CHAPTER 14

Decision

D ecision is the final element of the Sandler qualifying process. Every decision someone makes—even the apparent decision not to make a decision—constitutes a cause set in motion, a preference of one chain of events over another.

From the salesperson's point of view, qualifying for decision is about learning how to ask the types of questions that uncover the details of the enterprise account's decision-making process. This kind of questioning will help you deal with buyers at all levels of the wide and diverse buyer network that enterprise accounts have.

SANDLER ENTERPRISE SELLING RULE

Nothing happens until someone makes a decision.

There are three possible outcomes when it comes to qualifying for decision.

1. If your qualifying work is fully completed and the opportunity fails to qualify, you exit the process.
2. If your qualifying work is not fully completed, you continue qualifying for decision until you can determine a clear qualification status.
3. If your qualifying work is fully completed and the opportunity qualifies, you move on to Stage Four, Solution Development.

> *"Never allow a person to tell you 'no' who doesn't have the power to say 'yes.'"*
>
> —Eleanor Roosevelt

Detective Work

Identifying the decision process in an enterprise opportunity takes some detective work. You have to be willing to ask the right people the right questions, and you have to keep pushing, subtly, to fill in all the gaps. Roadblocks along the way are likely. You must find a way to work around them—tactfully.

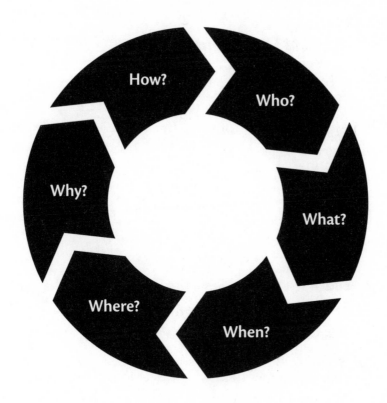

Every good news story has the six key elements: who, what, how, where, when, and why. (See Figure 14.1.) Taking this approach to determining an account's buying decision process is critical. The big challenge with enterprise accounts is that this information is likely to change over time, so you have to stay engaged.

The classic who, what, how, where, when, and why questions of a good reporter are important in every sales discussion. These questions and the discussions they initiate tend to be even more important in enterprise environments because there's more "news" you need to gather and understand in order to complete the Decision Step.

Two Kinds of Questions

To qualify for decision, you must gather good information. There are two kinds of questions you can use to gain some clarity on the decision process: open-ended questions that encourage the other person to paint with a broad stroke and element-specific questions designed to help the person fill in a specific information gap. By using these two questioning techniques effectively, you can learn more about internal constituencies and the competition.

Open-Ended Questions About the Decision Process

- Jessica, when your company makes a major purchase like the one we've been discussing, what process do you follow?
- When it comes to making a decision about investing in capital equipment, Tim, how does your company go about it?

Element-Specific Questions About the Decision Process

- You didn't mention who could veto the committee's decision, Chris. Who might that be?
- Brandon, you didn't mention when you'd like to have this decision made. What is the actual time frame?
- How will you ultimately decide who your partner will be, Juan?
- Yolanda, what will you need from me to be comfortable making a decision?
- Where in the organization are decisions like this finalized, Maria?

- Kate, why don't we schedule a conference call with the key players rather than relay information second hand?

Multiple Players, Longer Cycles

In the enterprise world, you must expect multiple players to take part in the decision process. Not only that, enterprise sales cycles are typically a good bit longer than those of traditional selling. You may learn that you have entered the process late. Some competitor may have gotten the jump on you, for whatever reason.

All of this is critical information, and some of it may require a fresh assessment of the Go/No-Go question. You may run into internal opposition you can't expect to overcome, or you may encounter competitors who are better positioned than you are that you didn't know you had.

Even if you do decide to move forward, you will need help. These kinds of problems can't be overcome without help from an ally within the target organization.

No Missing Pieces

So, what is qualification?

By now you should know the answer. Qualification is pain, budget, and decision—as confirmed for a specific, unique enterprise selling opportunity. One missing piece means there is no qualification.

If the problems can't be solved with your product or service, or the prospect doesn't have or is unwilling to make the necessary investments, or the prospect can't or won't share the process by which a decision will be made in a timely manner, the opportunity is disqualified.

On the other hand, if you have green lights in each of these areas, then you can move forward to Stage Four, Solution Development.

Remember: not everyone deserves your time and resources!

STAGE 4

Solution Development

Master the process for determining and crafting a solution for an enterprise prospect opportunity.

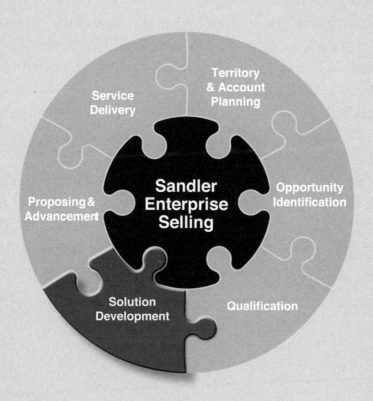

After all the work you have put in, you are now perfectly positioned to prepare and craft a product/service solution that uniquely qualifies your team to win the business.

Even if you are familiar with the Sandler Selling System, you will find that in this fourth stage of SES, there's much that is new. Here you will find many advanced tactics specifically designed for the enterprise selling environment that expands on fundamental Sandler concepts.

In chapter 15, **Refine the Position**, you'll focus on gathering and refreshing all of the relevant information to create a solid base of knowledge around an enterprise pursuit.

In chapter 16, **Pursuit Navigator**, you'll learn about this proprietary Sandler tool, which helps you determine as early as possible all the key Go/No-Go elements of the opportunity you are pursuing. You must confirm that you're in a deal that you can win. This chapter helps you make quality decisions about the significant investments you and your team are making.

In chapter 17, **Build and Form**, you'll learn what it takes to get the right people in the right seats on the right bus.

In chapter 18, **Compelling Themes**, you'll learn to create a powerful, customized, value-driven message.

In chapter 19, **Fingerprinting**, you'll master a critical enterprise selling principle: people are more likely to be persuaded by their own words than by your words.

CHAPTER 15

Refine the Position

This section begins with the concept of refining the position, which is a key element of solution development.

You have done your initial research into all of the relevant variables involving the prospect and the opportunity, and you have received the prospect's concurrence to proceed as a partner in the process. Now you are seriously engaged in the pursuit. Every day that you consciously decide to stay in it, it's costing your firm money, assets, and energy. So now, as Stage Four begins, you connect the key members of the selling team to share and/or refresh everything that you've learned about the opportunity up to this point.

SANDLER ENTERPRISE SELLING RULE

Gather the team and create a solid base of knowledge.

Connecting the selling team to evaluate a specific opportunity refines and expands your understanding of the prospect's needs, pains, and business requirements. This is the first step of enterprise solution development, the step that allows you to proceed in the pursuit with credibility and a solid base of knowledge.

The key areas to focus on follow.

Prospects and the Prospect Organization
- The cast of characters
- Organizational and individual needs
- Organizational and individual pains

Business Requirements
- The top 10 business requirement items (you'll learn about this in a moment)

Competition
- Competitive footprint
- Competitive history and relationships
- Competitive value proposition

Remember: enterprise selling, by definition, involves a team pursuit. Buyers buy in teams. You sell in teams. Given the strategic importance of any enterprise pursuit, it is absolutely critical that the entire selling team collaborate to complete this part of Stage Four. The whole is greater than the sum of its parts. You have to work as a team, and you have to evaluate all the most recent information collaboratively.

The LinkedIn Levers and Relationship Builder processes are repeated here at the beginning of Stage Four. Perhaps you're wondering: "Why would we redo something we already did in Stage Two?" The answer is simple: sales cycles in the enterprise world are long. People, plans, and priorities change over time. You have to be sure you have accurate information. These tools are dynamic resources that you update continually. They do not just sit on a shelf or in an e-folder.

Assume Nothing

When you refine the position, your team comes together to review, refresh, and update everything you know about this unique opportunity. Double check all your assumptions! If the business requirements or any other aspect of this opportunity have changed, the entire selling team needs to know.

Below, you'll find 10 critical business requirements you will need to double check as part of the refine-the-position team discussion.

1. The problem or pain to be addressed
2. The fundamental aspects of the new capability that is needed
3. Who the users will be and how they will use the new capability
4. How this new capability will best address the problem and pain
5. The benefits that will result
6. When the new capability is needed
7. The dependencies that need to be understood

8. The risks in this initiative
9. What is in and out of scope of the initiative?
10. The key assumptions being made

These elements increase in importance as the relationship moves forward. You'll learn more about each of them in Stage Six, Service Delivery.

The Competition, Revisited

It's time to revisit the key competitors and what you know of their value propositions. You're reusing the Positioning Tool here because it's focused completely on the competition. Again, these are resources you refresh over time—not tasks you complete once, cross off the list, and never revisit.

When you are up against sophisticated enterprise competition, you can rest assured that the competition's solutions have evolved over the course of the sales cycle, just as yours have. Make your very best evaluation. Know what you're up against.

If you haven't yet gathered all the current members of the selling team and comprehensively reviewed/confirmed all the essential information points mentioned in this chapter, you are not ready to proceed with the opportunity. This is one of the steps selling teams routinely skip, to their detriment.

CHAPTER 16

Pursuit Navigator

The Pursuit Navigator tool is a proprietary, structured team tool that helps you to determine as early in the process as possible the key Go/No-Go elements of an opportunity.

This understanding, based on the principles of risk identification and mitigation, will ensure that the opportunities you choose to pursue are highly likely to be won. All of the work you have done up to this point is comparable to the reconnaissance that a military unit does before a major battle. Now you need to determine whether it makes good strategic sense to launch the attack.

> ### SANDLER ENTERPRISE SELLING RULE
>
> *Early exit or early acceleration.*

In the enterprise world, it is just as important to know when to exit a current opportunity as it is to know when to begin a pursuit. Risk identification and mitigation are far more critical in the enterprise selling space than they are in traditional selling. In a traditional sale with a short selling cycle, having only a single point of contact within an account might not be a huge problem. But in an enterprise pursuit, it's a major element of risk that calls into question whether you should be pursuing the opportunity at all.

Ask yourself: "What are the hazards of continuing this pursuit?" There are multiple right answers to this question, including: losing major financial investments/time investments of multiple team members; the opportunity cost of not pursuing other activities; the risk of providing free consulting; even the possibility of inadvertently sharing sensitive or confidential information that might be picked up by a competitor. In this world, pursuing an opportunity out of force of habit—to prove something or to appease a member of the sales team—just doesn't make a lot of sense.

KNOW WHEN TO LEAVE THE PARTY

Based on the results of the Pursuit Navigator process, you can now make better, more appropriate Go/ No-Go decisions than you made previously. Knowing when to exit is just as important as knowing when to move forward. As strange as it may seem, reaching certainty in either direction will drive success and profitability for your organization.

The truth is that an enterprise sale is by definition a risky undertaking. You have to manage the risks intelligently. Enterprise pursuits are so expensive, take so long, and can change so fast, you must make smart Go/No-Go decisions at many points in the sales cycle. In a traditional sale, you generally make one decision about whether or not to pursue the business, and then you keep going until you get a decision. If you did that with every enterprise opportunity, you'd go bankrupt very quickly.

The Sandler Pursuit Navigator tool is all about making smart Go/No-Go decisions. It is not so much a one-time event as it is a way of doing business. Frankly, Go/No-Go is a mindset that must be integrated throughout the sales cycle. The tool helps craft winning solutions that can be delivered successfully and profitably. It can be summarized in five important words: *Early exit or early acceleration.*

All the major risks of pursuing a given opportunity in Table 16.1 are on the left side of the tool. The mitigations of the relevant risks are filled in on the right. Of course, you need people from different parts of the company if you are going to identify and fill in the right blanks.

There are three major categories: client issues, selling team issues, and financing/contract issues. Each issue is classified as either stable or requiring risk mitigation. If mitigation is required, the team identifies a strategy in the blank space and commits to identifying accountable members who will get back to the group with risk resolution plans, names, and deadline dates.

If the Pursuit Navigator process uncovers an unacceptable number of items needing risk mitigation, immediate action is required. Often, direct discussions with the prospect can bring about changes in the proposed structure of the deal that will mitigate or even eliminate the risk. If the prospect is not willing to make changes to the opportunity that will mitigate the risk, a decision must be made to either shut down the pursuit or to proceed with full knowledge and acceptance of the possible adverse consequences.

In most cases, being clear with a prospect about the reasoning behind pulling out of a pursuit is the best strategy. In other cases, business judgment may dictate that the true reason should remain confidential. The Pursuit Navigator also provides the basis for an "opportunity postmortem" exercise if the deal is lost, which is covered in a later chapter.

Look at Table 16.1 to see how this important enterprise selling tool works.

RISK FACTOR	MITIGATION STRATEGY
The client does not have a clear understanding of its responsibilities.	
We do not have multi-level client relationships.	*Sales, Delivery & Executive teams have targeted functional counterparts for relationship building. Report due back from DL, RT & GH by 8/15.*
The true buyers have not been involved in our discussions.	*Delivery team is engaging with direct functional users in relationship-building process to verify requirements. Report due back from RT by 8/8.*
The client uses multiple vendors delivering services similar to ours.	*Sales team responsible for gauging client satisfaction of Tetley and Tec-Alliance as primary competitors. Value props and snapshot due to be reported back from DL by 8/1.*
The client has doubts about our proposed solution.	
Failure in this deal will derail other key business we have with the client.	*Sales teams, via DL, to report back by 8/8 on insulating our current "Invest-T" project business with Finance Dept.*
The client is unwilling to communicate clearly and frequently.	

The Pursuit Navigator is a structured team process to help you determine as early in solution development as possible all the important elements to drive smart Go/No-Go decisions. The operative word there is *team*. This tool brings together all of the relevant stakeholders from the selling organization to make a Go/No-Go determination. Representatives may be from sales, legal, accounting, marketing, delivery, executive management, and so on.

A True Story

One selling team, an enterprise resource planning (ERP) services firm we'll call *Malafortuna,* had invested a significant amount of money developing a new division that was designed to sell into larger clients. They had a $6 million opportunity with a major player, a Fortune 2000 consumer products firm.

The Malafortuna team only performed a cursory Go/No-Go analysis on this pursuit. The analysis was not extensive enough to address the complexities of a prospect of this size or a deal of this magnitude. To make matters worse, they sent in a bid that was far too low. Essentially, they were trying to buy their first big account so the portfolio would look better and they could generate referrals. The team received what sounded like good news: they had won the business. Shortly after that notification, though, they ran into some significant issues with contract terms. Suddenly they realized this huge new client was expecting significant shared risk—a rather common issue in deals of this size and gravity. But the sales lead did not know that.

A daunting system of penalties was built into the bid. The seller had assumed they could finesse these points in the post-bid phase as they had with smaller clients in the past. "We'll handle that later," the sales lead had assured the CEO when asked, months earlier, about the troubling contract language. Not the right response to a red flag of that magnitude!

There were a number of issues Malafortuna simply could not overcome during the sophisticated, intense negotiation phase that followed. They were battling against a seasoned corporate legal team that knew how to handle situations like this. Ultimately, their award was rescinded. The business was given to a competitor. Had Malafortuna addressed the significant contract issues in the Go/No-Go analysis early on in the pursuit, they would have either resolved them or made a conscious decision that they should exit. If they had exited, they could have redeployed their assets, gotten their first big client somewhere else, and avoided some major expenses in terms of time, attention, lost opportunities and, of course, money.

There Is No Halfway

The Pursuit Navigator tool helps in the identification and crafting of relevant risk-mitigation actions. If you can identify and plot a way to deal with the issues, that's great! Proceed with confidence.

But if you can't mitigate the risk, it's highly likely that you should exit the process. Even one unmitigated risk means the deal is probably unwinnable or would result in a piece of business you might come to regret winning. Sometimes getting out is a gift because you don't waste critical resources like time, energy, attention, and money.

There are circumstances when, even if the risk cannot be mitigated, you might still decide to proceed. The continuation of the pursuit, though, would have to be made with full knowledge of the calculated risk. You would create defense strategies and comprehensive future mitigation plans. Assuming your company was in a position to do so, you would proceed at risk—forewarned and forearmed.

In the enterprise world, there is no halfway. If you are not 100 percent committed to a pursuit, others likely are. You will probably lose—and losses can be very expensive in this world.

The Pursuit Navigator isn't something you should do once in a while. It's got to be a way of doing business, day in and day out. It's got to be part of your enterprise selling culture.

If you haven't yet conducted an in-depth Pursuit Navigator session involving multiple internal stakeholders from different parts of your organization, you are not ready to proceed with the enterprise opportunity. This is one of the steps selling teams routinely skip, to their detriment. It typically requires coaching and facilitation.

CHAPTER 17

Build and Form

So where are you now in the enterprise sales process? You have successfully completed the first three stages, you have refreshed all of your information about the pursuit, and you have followed the Pursuit Navigator process to confirm that you truly are in a "Go" status with this opportunity.

These items are not always in a rigid sequence. In many situations and organizations, the proposal team may have already been partially formed at this point. Whether that's true or not, though, there does come a point where you have to formally identify and convene the team that will pursue this specific opportunity. That's what "build and form" is all about.

This chapter is about creating a formal team, with a charter of advancing one clearly identified opportunity. It's about getting the right people in the right seats on the right bus.

The build and form phase begins with the assembly of this proposal team. Following are some principles to bear in mind as you put this team together.

- **Start early.** Start thinking, early on, about the team you want to field for this specific opportunity. Even if a presentation has not yet been requested, you should still be preparing to identify the team members with the relevant skills and experience to drive the pursuit to a win.

- **Identify the proposal manager.** This person directs the team's activities, brings team members on board, and oversees all positions, functions, and activities related to the pursuit. Typically, the proposal manager has deep subject matter expertise or may be the person with the deepest experience in dealing with this particular account.

- **Add the relevant internal and external pursuit team members.** These should be people who have been engaged up to this point and will remain with those joining as new members. Your goal is to assemble team members who have both the commitment and the motivation to see the effort through and to win the business. The majority of the positions on the team should involve full-time members of the selling organization from various teams, but other resources could include outside parties contracted on the pursuit (technical writers, editors, etc.) and possibly even external business partners. Outsiders on the team should have no competitive interest or relationship to the target account other than their ties with you.

Close-Up: Possible Internal Team Members

Following is a list of internal areas from which you can draw members of the pursuit team. How many of these different groups can you ensure are represented?

- Legal
- Contracts
- Accounting
- Finance
- IT
- Project/program management
- Marketing
- Sales
- Service lines
- Practice groups
- Executive management
- Representatives from parent companies, subsidiaries, etc.

Close-Up: Possible External Team Members

Next, it's time to consider the external partners who would be involved. These business, channel, and alliance partners can have huge stakes in pursuits and can play major roles. They and other external assets are often involved in enterprise proposal teams. Of course, you have to make certain that all the logistical bases are covered, which means setting up non-disclosure agreements and non-compete agreements for the people from the external partnership groups who form part of your greater team. Again, which resources would you see engaging in an enterprise pursuit?

- Subcontractors
- Writers
- Editors
- Graphic designers/architects
- Alliance partners
- Channel partners
- Reviewers
- Industry experts
- Subject matter experts
- Alumni

CHOOSE THE TEAM CAREFULLY

The higher the quality of your internal and external team members, the greater your chance of success. There is often a temptation to engage resources simply because they have the time and the availability. This is a bad idea.

Sometimes the resources who are available are not those whose talents and experience align with a specific need. Hold out for the right team.

RACI, Again

We covered the helpful RACI accountability system (responsible, accountable, consulted, informed) in Stage One, with the Growth Account Booster. Now, with a proposal team, it's even more important to have total clarity when it comes to roles, responsibilities, and communication protocols.

Remember, some people on the proposal team may be committed to the pursuit full time, while others are only involved part time and must balance their contributions with other functions and other responsibilities. Because of that dynamic, RACI is a vitally important resource for the proposal team. Now that you know this system, use it!

CHAPTER 18

Compelling Themes

It's time to revisit the concept of the value proposition.

You'll remember that you started to work on value propositions way back in Stage One. But at that point the value proposition was targeted to the territory as a whole. You kept the theme of value top of mind throughout the process and remained laser focused on the question of identifying the value you could ultimately bring to the market. In this chapter, the value proposition evolves to the opportunity level with themes that are compelling to specific individual decision makers because they are directly aligned to their specific needs and pains.

SANDLER ENTERPRISE SELLING RULE

Create a powerful, customized, value-driven message.

The evolution of the customized value proposition is one of the things that makes enterprise selling different from every other kind of selling. Back in Stage One, you'll recall, you explored what you do well, seeking favorable conditions for a pursuit, and building the territory value propositions that addressed the territory as a whole. Those value propositions were in your 30-second commercial. They were key parts of the SES tools you have used throughout the program.

Now you must take it to another level. It's time to create a highly customized value proposition for one pursuit that you've made a conscious decision to engage and keep engaged. This value proposition must be completely client-focused.

Each of the following customized value propositions was developed with a specific opportunity and a specific problem, or pain, in mind.

- **For a global on-demand printing services firm's customized value proposition for an international legal services firm:** "Our Glodax local printing capability allows us to print on-demand in 120 countries, meeting contract and project deadlines, and cutting printing costs by 74 percent."
- **For an Internet marketing firm's customized value proposition for a major pharmaceuticals firm:** "Our Duneazer web-based service allows us to leverage the Internet to increase your speed to market and cut your product launch marketing costs in half."
- **For a heavy equipment distribution network's value proposition for a mining firm:** "Our Kopidrill regional distribution network allows us to deliver

tungsten carbide rock drill bits in emergency situations anywhere in North America within four hours
of order, increasing operational safety levels, minimiz-
ing downtime, reducing liability, and cutting project
delay costs by 12 percent on average."

These value propositions connect all the dots. Not only do
they deliver clarity for clients and prospects, they also build
confidence in salespeople, who can confidently and authenti-
cally associate client pains to their own organizational value.

REMEMBER THE VALUE ARROWS

*Each customized value proposition you develop must
directly or indirectly address all four of these elements:*

When we have this [name the product/service]...

...we will be able to...

*..., which means that our
organization will benefit by...*

...and we'll measure the improvements through...

Setting the Stage

The customized value proposition you develop is unique. It
has to set the stage for everything you do and say from this
point forward in the pursuit.

You are going to pepper the proposal and your talk tracks with specific key words from the value proposition that you know resonates with this specific client. These key words remind your contacts of the clear alignment between their pain and your solutions.

These repeated words are *value links*, and you have to know what they are ahead of time. You must build them into the value proposition and all the rest of your communication with this prospect.

Value links bring to life the value proposition and the rest of your communication with the client. When you use these words in themed sound-bite messages, you can convey your customized value proposition powerfully in short bursts across multiple communication points. But you can't do that unless you build them into the customized value proposition first.

Examples of Value Link Words

Some examples of powerful value link words you can build into your value proposition and then repeat strategically follow:

- Responsiveness
- Dependability
- Performance
- Track record
- Experience
- Flexibility
- Scalability
- Sustainability
- Measurability

- Low cost
- Cost effectiveness
- Percentage cost savings
- Speed to market
- Safety

Use Them Everywhere

You can use value links in both written and verbal communication. They will seamlessly establish the relevance of your solution and, in turn, reiterate and reinforce your value.

Just like the customized value propositions in which they appear, value links must be created with a specific prospect's pain/problem in mind. They should be shared with all members of the selling team to enrich talk tracks and drive client alignment.

KNOW YOUR THEME

"Not knowing your theme until you're finished is like using a scalpel to turn a kangaroo into Miss Universe."

—David G. Allen, "Why Theme Still Matters."
(Article published May 17, 2013, at www.authordavid.com
/theme-matters-in-entertainment.)

CHAPTER 19

Fingerprinting

This chapter is all about gaining client feedback. It's a simple concept, yet it's often ignored.

In addition to keeping the lines of communication open so that you can learn about changing developments on the buying side of the pursuit, fingerprinting helps you make sure you are on the right track. There is real power in sharing with trusted contacts the themes, strategies, and tactics of your planned solution. Your prospects will have opinions about these, and they will share those opinions. Supporting and integrating this process of sharing information is called "gaining the client's fingerprints" on your proposed course of action.

You don't want to spend the tremendous amount of time, energy, and effort required in an enterprise pursuit only to learn you have lost the deal because you've been developing your solution in a vacuum. Regardless of how effective you are as an organization in all of the research you conduct to understand the target organization's needs and pains, there is no substitute for gaining direct feedback about your plans from the people making or influencing the ultimate decision.

> ### SANDLER ENTERPRISE SELLING RULE
>
> *People are more likely to be persuaded by their own words than by yours.*

This process of asking for feedback is actually a pretty basic element of human interaction. Would you buy expensive gifts for your friends without having any idea as to how they would feel about it? Would you make that kind of an investment without bothering to get firsthand understanding as to whether your purchase will be well-received? Of course you wouldn't. When in doubt, ask people what they think.

That's the whole point of fingerprinting—gaining client input on what you're doing, at every possible step of the process. Even though fingerprinting is highlighted at this point in the SES program, you'll see from this chapter that it makes sense to use it regularly throughout the enterprise sales cycle.

Coaches and Sponsors

How important is it to have a coach or sponsor within the target organization to guide you?

You guessed it—it's absolutely essential. These are supportive internal guides within the target organization. It is vitally important to have coaches and other client supporters to whom you can turn for advice and input. If you don't have that kind of relationship in place, you should not be surprised when you lose the opportunity.

Of course, situations do exist where there are barriers to getting information directly from client contacts. In the real world, you may run into rules that you will be required to follow in some enterprise pursuits that limit or exclude direct collaboration on your proposal.

But here's the good news. If you have supporters in the client cast of characters (and of course you must), then you can find a way to get reliable, useful information via informal conversations. Yes, you do have to understand the supply chain structure, and yes, you do have to follow the rules. But you can and should have offline conversations to gain the critical fingerprinting input you need.

Always be prepared to tailor your fingerprinting approach. If the client feels uncomfortable in any way about anything, do whatever it is your coach feels necessary. Then share what you discover with the overall pursuit team.

What you discover in these fingerprinting conversations can make the difference between winning and losing. That's not so surprising. After all, it's tough for people to say "no" to an idea they helped create.

The Truth, the Whole Truth, and Nothing but the Truth

Fingerprinting is all about having a good open-ended approach. One caution for these conversations—don't ask leading questions! You do not want to maneuver the client into providing you a particular answer. You want the truth because the truth is what's going to determine whether you win or you lose. The truth will help you figure out what works and what doesn't. The truth will determine whether you produce a customized client-focused offer or ultimately make a decision to withdraw from the opportunity.

STAGE 5

Proposing and Advancement

Learn the process for preparing and delivering client-centric responses that set the path forward.

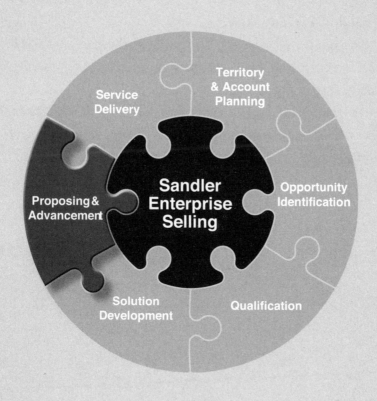

The intention of this stage is not to focus on the details of building your proposal-development skills. Most of the companies that participate in Sandler Training already have effective processes in this area. Instead, the focus is on the critical role of the sales team in enterprise proposal development and the voice of the customer, two important and connected themes. You'll also explore how you can ensure advancement and continued progress, regardless of the client's decision in the selection process.

In chapter 20, **Developing the Response**, you'll focus on crafting a superior response for the business you've earned the right to win.

In chapter 21, you'll get ready to deliver a focused **Proposal and Presentation**.

In chapter 22, you'll look closely at the prospect's **Selection** process, and find out how to turn any outcome you receive into a win.

In chapter 23, you'll cover the **Agreement and Transition** period, and learn how to turn the *yes* you just received into a seamless transition to a fair and workable contract.

CHAPTER 20

Developing the Response

I t's time for you to actively develop the proposal. Depending on the complexity of the pursuit and the requirements of the target organization, the depth and detail to which proposal processes extend may include areas that drill deeper than those listed below. However, whatever process you choose must at the very least encompass the following elements:

- Strategy review
- Completion of business case
- ROI development
- Reference validation
- Completion of cost/pricing
- Finalizing the solution
- Developing the draft
- Draft review

> ### SANDLER ENTERPRISE SELLING RULE
>
> *Bid on the business you've earned the right to win.*

Why is it so important for the sales lead to be engaged in each of these areas and have a deep understanding of what's going on in all eight? Because in enterprise selling, which can become quite complex, someone on the selling side has to know what the whole response looks like and someone must be accountable. If the left hand doesn't know what the right hand is doing, the odds of failure are high—and failure is expensive.

When proposal responses are led by nonsales resources, the voice of the customer can sometimes be hard to hear since the focus can shift to the technical or operational nature of the solution. There may be an organizational temptation to recycle assets that are not targeted to the needs and pains you have uncovered in this specific pursuit. If you are the sales lead, you must counteract this tendency.

To keep this from happening, some organizations even keep an empty chair representing the client being pursued in every proposal meeting. That chair provides a constant visual reminder that you are doing what you are doing for one reason and one reason only: to satisfy the customer—the most important person in the room.

In order to create a response that vividly incorporates the voice of the customer, you must do the following.

- Keep the client's needs and pains at the forefront of your thinking. Your organization's capabilities and/

or past experiences are not the starting point for these discussions. The discussion should begin with the client.

- Focus on this unique client with whom you are dealing. Although you should take advantage of lessons learned from previous pursuits, you must not reuse archived assets that are not targeted to the relevant needs and pains you have uncovered.

Leading the Response: Eight Tips for a Powerful Client-centric Proposal

The sales lead has the responsibility to ensure that the voice of the customer is always heard loud and clear as the response is developed. If you are the sales lead, you must do the following.

1. Ensure that client-centric guidance and questions are consistently brought to bear throughout the proposal-development process.
2. Leave an empty chair at all of your planning meetings. This seat belongs to the customer, who is the most important person in the room.
3. Double-check that you have assigned the right human resources to the proposal development and the ultimate delivery as opposed to those people who are simply available.
4. Utilize references and/or case studies that are fresh and pertinent to the specific client situation.
5. Ensure that the team crafts a truly customized solution as opposed to employing delivery techniques

previously used that may not be as relevant as is required.

6. Use client fingerprinting for confirmation and concurrence at every critical point as opposed to spending lots of time and energy crafting solutions that only you feel will resonate.

7. Integrate a customized value proposition and value links that directly match the client's relevant needs and pains.

8. Identify and embed relevant vertical and client-specific verbiage throughout the response.

The Monkey's Paw

Have you ever heard of a "monkey's paw"? In nautical circles, this is a special knot that weights the end of a heaving line—which is the rope you throw across the water to moor your boat at a wharf. One end of the rope is tied securely to the boat. The other end, the end you throw toward the wharf, is meant to bring you safely into shore. The whole purpose of this knot is to catch hold of the metal mooring-point built into the wharf, something that's virtually impossible to do with a rope that has no knot tied at the unsecured end.

The monkey's paw is a comparatively small knot with a huge impact. That little knot gets you from the open waters into your chosen landing spot–the most important part of the journey.

The principle of the monkey's paw is relevant not just to sailors but also to salespeople. In the world of enterprise selling, a monkey's paw is a little, easy-to-gain agreement that sets up a big partnership with the target organization. It takes you off the open sea, which can be chaotic and unpredictable, and brings you safely into harbor.

Sandler has trained salespeople to use a monkey's paw process for many years. It's extremely effective for situations where you want to launch quickly, especially with an organization that hasn't worked with you before. In the enterprise world, the monkey's paw plays a particularly crucial role.

Should You Propose a Monkey's Paw?

With a monkey's paw approach, you attempt to close on a small piece of business in order to convert a prospect to a client. You choose to work for the larger piece of business later.

Whether and when to propose such an initial engagement are important strategic decisions. These decisions must be based on your understanding of all the relevant factors in this pursuit, which are likely to include:

- Client culture
- Competitive strategies
- Client need for quick results
- Funding limitations
- Client need for verification of your approach

Different Kinds of Monkey's Paws

The monkey's paw has many variations in the enterprise selling world. Below, you will find a list of some of the most common. Understand that different organizations use different names to describe these variations. Make sure you understand which is which, along with which will resonate best with a particular client.

- **Proof-of-Concept (POC):** A small exercise to prove the viability of a solution or to show how a product/service will deliver.
- **Prototype:** Expansion on POC with a more complete implementation allowing deeper analysis and verification.
- **Pilot:** A small program designed to prove how a large-scale initiative would work in practice.
- **Trial:** A temporary offering to allow for use of a product/service prior to a commitment for long-term acquisition.
- **Quick-Start:** Speedy kick-off of an initiative with structured milestones and specific results to be achieved in short order.

These initial vehicles can deliver quick verification of your solution and also provide clarity regarding the requirements and the practical application of your approach. Yet, you must proceed with caution. These types of engagement starters prove the validity of the "high risk, high reward" mantra. Successful execution typically means clear sailing to winning the overall bid, while failure usually means that you are done for good. Propose the option that will allow your organization to shine.

Two True Stories

Natalie was a very successful salesperson working for a company we'll call *J-Top Consulting*. Over a three-year period, her average sale was well over $2 million. Natalie knew that her product/service was strong, and she was confident in her closing ability. Her pipeline was filled with many larger opportunities, some of which were worth north of $5 million. "Life," she liked to say, "was good."

Over the years, though, something had started to slip. Natalie had moved exclusively towards larger sales, leaving the smaller sales behind because they took too much time and energy away from her "elephant hunting." Over time, though, she found she was losing more and more deals she should have been winning. She was spending months and months chasing opportunities that seemed well qualified, only to lose them at the finish line—not a good pattern in any selling environment, and a deeply troubling one in the enterprise world.

Why was this happening? Her competitors on the deals she was losing were closing smaller arrangements in the $50,000 to $60,000 range, giving the prospects a lower decision point and less financial risk. Not only that, decision makers had an opportunity to try out the solutions before they had to buy a longer-term commitment. That sense of safety was something that appealed to the clients. Natalie lost more and more business because of her "elephant hunting" strategy. Three years went by before she recognized that a foot-in-the-door strategy would serve her and her clients better.

Paige was a salesperson who worked in a different division of J-Top Consulting. For her first few years on the job, she was moderately successful. Her average sale was in the $750,000 range. Her clients were uniformly pleased with the high, measurable ROI that followed Paige's engagements. Once she had a client, it was usually easy for her to renew that client for future engagements.

But Paige wanted to expand her client base. She knew that prospects with whom she hadn't yet worked didn't have the sort of trust in her experience that her current clients did. She needed a strategy that would allow her to "get the customer off the street"—to start the business relationship.

She began offering $50,000 studies as entry-point vehicles. She knew that the people she was calling typically had the authority to approve deals below $100,000. This pricing made the decisions relatively easy. Paige bypassed the committees that were mandatory for the larger decisions—and she was able to shortcut the long sales cycles and in-depth reviews of the bigger projects. The $50,000 studies allowed her to move from vendor to partner quickly and easily. She formed the relationships needed with those who were ultimately going to make a larger relationship possible.

Her sales cycle shortened dramatically. It took her less than half the time to close the $50,000 deal as it did to close the $500,000 engagement. She had an 86 percent extension rate for those who went through the smaller sale. Within a year, Paige was the number one salesperson at J-Top.

Previewing the Solution

By this point, you've put a great deal of time and effort into the pursuit. You have a responsibility to get and incorporate the feedback of your coaches in the account.

You've already read about the powerful benefits of gaining client fingerprints on whatever you plan. Now you should seek the opportunity to "pre-present" the highlights of your proposal to your best client contacts if it is at all possible to do so. This pre-present session would typically be informal and should be driven and structured by the prospect's insights and suggestions.

In certain situations, there may be organizational restrictions prohibiting pre-proposals. Such prohibitions, of course, must be respected. Lacking an actual pre-present, generating fingerprinting feedback from clients at this point, even only on minor details, is the next-best option. It may be all you need.

You already know that you must be sensible and sensitive in terms of what you request and do in seeking client feedback. Be smart. Do not take any risks that could potentially sidetrack or sabotage your opportunity.

DON'T GO IT ALONE

Remember: Fingerprinting is still a priority.

Listen to the voice of the customer, develop the response, and seek the opportunity to preview your solution.

CHAPTER 21

Proposal and Presentation

The enterprise presentation requires more preparation and practice than presentations in traditional selling.

As mentioned earlier, the intention of this stage is not to improve your proposal development skills. It's important to remember, though, that this is not a "cookie cutter" event, but an ongoing team endeavor requiring close collaboration across work groups. A vitally important tool during this period of preparation and practice is the RACI—responsible, accountable, consulted, informed—accountability process, which was emphasized in the formation of the team and which has special significance during the preparation to present. Clarity in roles and responsibilities is still critical.

Two Proposal Situations

A formal presentation typically takes one of two forms. Either the presentation accompanies the delivery of the written proposal, or it is requested by the client after the proposal is delivered. The latter typically is a result of a "narrowing of the field," in which a larger group of proposal-submitting firms is cut down to a manageable number. For example, six proposals may have been invited and received by the prospect, but three may have been dismissed as unacceptable. The remaining three proposal-submitting firms would be "down-selected" or invited in to present, usually in a "best and final" format.

Typically, a live presentation will either be delivered at the time you pass along your written proposal or it will be requested after the proposal has been delivered. Obviously, you want to know ahead of time which of these two situations to expect. That's part of qualifying the decision process.

Identifying all the attendees at the formal presentation is absolutely critical. Your audience likely will include new members of the buyer network who have not been involved up to this point. Often, business users and/or executive management may make a first appearance at this presentation. Work with your coaches to determine the best strategies for addressing their issues.

The Presentation Rehearsal

Rehearsing for a key presentation is the ultimate in pre-call planning. All of the traditional call-planning elements apply. This type of preparation, however, is highly focused and unique to the enterprise world. Its key components are covered here.

A great deal of detail goes into actually planning and conducting rehearsals and presentations. Often, there is little time to prepare or rehearse to deliver the presentation. Nonetheless, you must make the best possible use of the time available.

The first element in the rehearsal process is to ensure that all the people involved in the presentation are refreshed regarding any updated information. Significant time may have passed since the proposal was delivered, and team members may have been redeployed to other initiatives. If so, they need to be brought back into the loop. Updated information should be provided on key topics such as:

- Remaining competition
- Value proposition impact
- Status of key buyers
- Agenda for the presentation
- Roles and responsibilities of presentation team members
- Presentation logistics
- Presentation theme and strategy

Team Leadership

A team leader must be chosen for the presentation team and for these rehearsal sessions. Quite often, this will be the sales lead, the person with the strongest relationship to the account. The leader could also be a senior member of the delivery team or another selling team member well-connected to the account or with unique qualifications regarding the solution. All other factors being equal, you should choose the leader whose presence is most likely to secure the deal.

Confidence and Conviction

A good rehearsal helps presenters build confidence and conviction in their roles and allows participants to practice handouts and/or demonstrations. Rehearsing helps people get comfortable with their material and gain confidence in their ability to perform.

Fine-Tuning

The rehearsal gives team members a chance to fine-tune their strategy for the meeting. For instance, the team as a whole should discuss the best ways to identify and address the competition's value propositions, as well as how to deal with the competition's supporters on the client team. These are not points you want to improvise during the presentation.

Environment

As best as you can, try to replicate the actual physical layout of the presentation venue in the rehearsal. Practicing in a room of similar size, similar layout, and with a similar technology platform will make the rehearsal more realistic and effective.

Time

Timing is a critical element of the presentation. Don't exceed the time contract that will be made with the buying team. Prepare and rehearse to finish under the allotted time.

Contingency Planning

At the end of your rehearsal and critique sessions, take time to consider how you could cut your presentation to a "bare bones" version if you were required to do so. Buying teams often schedule several meetings in a row, and your expected time allotment may be cut short. Based on your position in the sequence, you may be required to pare your presentation back in the interest of time. If that happens, you want to know, ahead of time, what your backup plan is going to be. Be professional. Be prepared.

Your Presentation Rehearsal Checklist

Review this checklist now and use it later to evaluate a presentation rehearsal. Feel free to add specific items relevant to your situation.

- ☐ Arrive early and completely prepared with all relevant materials.
- ☐ Thank the group for the opportunity to present.
- ☐ Set your up-front contract and be sure to reconfirm the time allotted.
- ☐ Affirm your commitment and interest in serving the client.
- ☐ Clearly state the roles of each presentation team member.

- [ ] Seek the expectations of the group and set those you have planned.
- [ ] Focus, from the start, on the client's needs and pains and gain concurrence.
- [ ] Present your capability in the direct context of the clear value proposition.
- [ ] Transition effectively from one presenter/presentation to the next.
- [ ] Use slides to illustrate points—do not read from them in a scripted fashion.
- [ ] Illustrate energy and passion in the presentation.
- [ ] Use action phrases: "We do this," instead of, "We plan to do this."
- [ ] Use tonality, volume, and pauses effectively to deliver impact.
- [ ] Be aware of body language in terms of hand usage, pacing, gestures, etc.
- [ ] Take the client's temperature at key points before proceeding.
- [ ] Smile and use eye contact and head nodding as client affirmation.
- [ ] Speak crisply, without saying "um" or "uh."
- [ ] In Q&A, be sure the most appropriate team member answers.
- [ ] Review expectations in closing.
- [ ] Reaffirm your commitment and interest in serving the client.
- [ ] Seek clarity on next steps.
- [ ] Thank the group in closing.
- [ ] Beat your time contract.

Your Rehearsing Routine

Think about your last formal presentation. Answer "yes" or "no" to each of the following questions about that presentation.

Yes | No   I identified ahead of time all the prospect decision makers who would be in attendance at the formal presentation.

Yes | No   I researched each of the prospect decision makers I identified via LinkedIn.

Yes | No   I spent at least one hour rehearsing the presentation.

Yes | No   I informally previewed our solution with the prospect.

Yes | No   I took part in a practice presentation with my colleagues.

Yes | No   I received feedback and critique on my practice presentation.

Yes | No   My practice presentation included colleagues from other functional areas of my organization.

Even one "no" answer is cause for concern.

Delivering the Presentation

After completing an effective presentation rehearsal, you are prepared to deliver the presentation. The presentation team is assembled and prepared with all members having clearly defined roles. As mentioned earlier, a key executive from your organization should be present to convey the commitment that your firm has to the client and the initiative. Typically, a short opening speech by the executive will suffice to verbalize that commitment. Remember: it's absolutely critical that all members of the presentation team who stand in front of the client have clearly stated roles and responsibilities. Parading people without clear roles in front of a client in a presentation event is unacceptable and will be viewed negatively by the client.

Your Proposal Structure

There are many different ways to deliver an effective enterprise proposal, but your presentation structure should probably end up looking like this:

1. **Opening:** High-impact up-front contract
2. **Set the Stage:** Review of the value proposition
3. **Introductions:** Clarity around roles and responsibilities
4. **Delivery:** Clear and direct delivery with value links throughout
5. **Transitions:** Seamless and sensible transfers between speakers
6. **Recap:** Review of hard-hitting points with summary of strong value
7. **Closure:** Defined commitment for action items and next steps

Following Up

When and how you follow up is incredibly important in the enterprise world. It is hard to overemphasize the importance of prompt, personalized follow-up with each member of the buying group.

If it is permitted to do so, the key executive or team leader should reach out to each buying-side participant, typically via e-mail, within 24 hours after the presentation. The individual thank-you notes should review any action items that came out of the presentation, expectations, and ways in which your product or service addresses the client's pains.

Be certain that these messages are customized to each individual buyer. After all of the time and the effort spent to this point, there's simply no excuse for underwhelming a client by sending a boilerplate thank-you note. If you have an individualized point you can make with each, that's very effective. But even if you don't, be sure that each message is different.

MOVE THE DISCUSSION FORWARD

Your follow-up communications must reference the specific action items that come out of the presentation.

Pre-Presentation Crisis

To close this important chapter, here is an important pre-presentation hypothetical shared with participants in the SES program. After having submitted your written proposal a week ago, as required by the target organization, your firm was chosen as one of three vendors to provide a 90-minute presentation two weeks from today. Your presentation team has been assembled and the team leader has been selected. This morning, in a conversation with a key client contact, you learned that your written approach was well done, but one of the remaining competitors provided a price 15 percent lower than yours and a project delivery timeframe 20 percent shorter than yours. Additionally, two members of the buying team had the impression that your firm is "difficult to work with." Your client contact was called away to an important meeting before you could get any more information. Making reasonable assumptions, how will you proceed in terms of your preparation? Your strategy? Your tactics?

List your ideas on a separate sheet of paper.

Good answers will vary, but a "right answer" might include the following.

Your chief contact within the account may find a way to get you access to the two members of the buying team who have formed a negative opinion. You may be able to figure out what lies behind their comments and conduct another fingerprinting session. If you can't get access to those two members of the buying team, perhaps your internal coach can get information for you as to why the two contacts feel the way they do. In addition, you could ask your chief contact whether the competitor's solution was actually similar to yours or something that's been pared down. Are they comparing apples to apples? In order to address the pricing and timeframe issues you face, you might ask for the chance to brainstorm with your chief contact about a smaller-scaled, more aggressive "proof of concept" offering that could show the competitor's cost and time savings to be illusory or overstated. Or you might determine—too late for your tastes, perhaps—that your planning simply was not as effective as it should have been, and that it doesn't make sense to keep investing money, time, and effort in this opportunity.

CHAPTER 22

Selection

L et's start by looking at the worst-case scenario when it comes to the target organization's selection process. What happens if you lose the deal?

It's a little surprising how many enterprise sellers don't know the best answer to that question. If you've gotten this far and you came close, you want to consider playing for the long term. In most cases, you don't want to simply disappear off the target organization's radar screen. Instead, you want to maintain all the good will and relationships you've built up to get to this point—and maybe even look for an opportunity to snatch victory from the jaws of defeat. Last but not least, you want to learn what happened.

SANDLER ENTERPRISE SELLING RULE

You win, or you learn.

Remember: There Are No "Anvil Sales"

The enterprise world is about streams of transactions over time in long-term relationships. You compete to win, but you know the reality that losing happens. It's expensive. It hurts. But it happens. The question is: How do you turn a loss into a win?

The good news is that there are no "anvil sales" in the enterprise world—no solitary, one-time sales of a product that lasts more or less forever, like there were back in the day when people sold anvils to blacksmiths. There is always another day. You and your firm will be judged by the way that you conduct yourselves if you are not chosen. You need to start by having the mindset that a loss is the first step to a win. That win may come sooner than you think. The first thing to do upon hearing of a loss is to thank the prospect organization and the individual buyers for having given your firm the opportunity to pursue their business. Showing your sincerity, respect, and professionalism at this point is critical.

Your organization will be judged, not so much by the loss, but by how you react to the loss. Of course, you will feel disappointment in losing. Yet it's important to accept that this loss may well be the first step in winning the next deal.

Victory from the Jaws of Defeat

Losses can quickly be softened by opportunities to subcontract under winning firms. Especially in the services world, winning firms may not have the resources to ramp up as quickly as a new engagement requires and may need quality subcontracting. If you have handled the loss professionally and are viewed that way by the client and the winning firm, you may have a smaller win that will help ease the pain of the bigger loss. You may even soon be returning the favor to your competitor/partner on a deal that you have won.

Of course, this is not always feasible or even desirable, but it should not be overlooked as a viable way to generate revenue and grow your business. These opportunities are available not only based on your delivery capability as a potential partner, but also on whether you and your firm are the kinds of partners with whom other firms would feel good about working.

Even If You Lose, Ask for the Meeting

After every loss, you should seek client feedback as to what you could have done better. Let's take a look at how you do that. Of course, you need to respect the moment. The truth is that scheduling a debriefing with a losing vendor is not likely to be high on the client's priority list as they work with the winning firm to kick off the new engagement. But you do want to stay on the radar screen, and you do want to stay grateful, upbeat, and professional at all times.

Not all clients will agree to a formal debriefing, but you should make every professional effort to see to it that one occurs. If the client will not agree to a debriefing meeting, do your best to gain the information needed through less formal means. While debriefing topics will be customized for each situation, the following is a suggested format of some of the basic items/questions that should be covered in the session.

- Which firm was selected as the winner?
- How many firms were considered?
- Was any scoring of the proposals done? If so, would the scores be available for review?
- Did the winning firm have the lowest price?
- Where did we fit in the price rankings?
- How were we viewed in terms of strengths and weaknesses?
- Was our solution acceptable from a technical/operational perspective?
- How did our solution compare to that of the winning firm?
- What was the clear differentiator for the winning firm?
- Did our response have a differentiator versus the others? If so, what was it?
- What was the primary reason the winner was selected?
- What was the primary reason we were not selected?
- What could we have done differently to be selected as the winner?
- What future opportunities would you see matching our capabilities?

After the results of the debriefing, the new information you have gained can help you rethink the account in terms of its viability as a prospect—and help you strategize a better way to pursue their business in the future if you choose to do so.

We Lost the Deal—Why?

The meeting to ask the client for following a loss is known as a *client debrief*. It's important, but it's not all you have to do. There is another critical event that must follow a loss: the *postmortem*.

The postmortem is an internal event that typically follows the client debriefing but may precede it. Even if the client debrief doesn't happen, the postmortem stands alone.

You already have your template for the postmortem in the Pursuit Navigator event that you conducted earlier. That session led you to conclude that this pursuit was a wise business decision and that you had minimized the risks in the opportunity and maximized your potential to win. But in the end, you lost. You must have missed something, or been wrong in one or more of your assumptions. That's why you convene this meeting: to review the work you did on the Pursuit Navigator and find out what it was that you missed.

The entire premise of the postmortem is to increase the likelihood that you win future deals by understanding what you might have done better in deals that you lost.

You win or you learn. Having lost, you can review those issues again in the postmortem and see exactly where your risk mitigation fell short.

CHAPTER 23

Agreement and Transition

Victory!

You've just been notified that you've won the business. This is where the real work begins.

To begin with, you will want to use that same Pursuit Navigator template discussed earlier to conduct a postmortem session designed to identify what you did well and perhaps not so well, even after a win. This will deliver more lessons learned and help ensure that you maximize the likelihood of winning again—with this client or with someone else. It's not a separate chapter because it's exactly the same process. Sometimes you win and you learn!

A True Story

A large document management, equipment, and services provider—we'll call them *PrintXX*—submitted a winning proposal for on-premise print management services for the corporate headquarters location of PRR Bank, a regionally based bank with 112 branches in a tristate area. While kicking off the new relationship, PrintXX requested a debriefing of their winning proposal. PRR shared their selection process, which involved the process of elimination to pare down from the list of four submitting vendors to the winner. In reviewing the grading of the selection criteria, it emerged that, while PrintXX was the clear winner, a key contact, PRR's VP of marketing, had voted for another vendor, RT Inc. Why?

The post-win analysis revealed that RT's full-color capabilities allowed for quicker turnaround for on-demand marketing jobs. Understanding this issue, PrintXX was able to meet with PRR's marketing department to better understand their unique needs. As a result, PrintXX restructured their processes and equipment configurations to address the marketing department's on-demand needs for color. This resulted in an increase of 15 percent in the variable revenues over the proposal dollar value for PrintXX and a savings of over $225,000 annually for PRR.

Stand Your Ground, Tactfully, and Professionally

You now have to move from verbal agreement to a fully executed contract that is fair to both sides. Your company was chosen for a reason. Now your job is to finalize that commitment as professionally and seamlessly as possible. Of course, you've earned the right to do that. Often, attorney-to-attorney communication will be necessary to streamline contract issues.

The Haze of Victory

What's the very first thing you would do if you won the lottery? Most people tell us that one of the first things they would do would be to tell a loved one.

There's a potential problem with that approach, though. Once you celebrate the windfall by pulling out your phone and telling your husband/wife/mother/father/son/daughter, etc., who else is going to know? Everybody! These days, big news makes it onto social media pretty quickly. All kinds of interesting things are going to start happening after that, not all of them conducive to your best interests. Maybe it makes sense to keep your cards close to the vest for a day or two—and call your financial advisor before you call anyone else.

What about in the enterprise world? Do you think that kind of thing ever happens after you get a verbal agreement? Telling one or two people about a big win, which then turns into having told everyone on Earth?

Yes!

That's called a poor decision after a big win. At all costs, avoid broadcasting your win until the contract is signed. Even if you don't put the news out on social media, someone else you talk to may—and that puts you in a horrible negotiating position. Celebrating early is a margin-killer.

POSTPONE THAT ONLINE UPDATE

"Do not rejoice over what has not yet happened."

—Egyptian Proverb

Countdown to Launch

As the contract structuring continues, it makes sense for the winning firm to begin preparations for the start of service. Making reasonable assumptions to proceed with your startup plan makes sense, but you should defer any significant financial and personnel commitments until you have signed contracts.

Below, you will find a helpful review of the key communications and the most important action items. Use it as a prekickoff checklist.

Before the Contract Is Finalized

Double check:

- Delivery team organization chart
- Roles and responsibilities
- Scope
- Engagement approach
- Goals/mission
- Management approach
- Schedule
- Deliverables
- Quality plan
- Work breakdown structure
- Acceptance procedures
- Status of reviews
- Assumptions
- Constraints
- Risk mitigation strategy
- Process/methodology

As you prepare for the project launch, the coinvolvement of sales and delivery team members in the crafting of the agreement is particularly important. This is how you lay the foundation for client satisfaction and account growth.

STAGE 6

Service Delivery

Master the process for developing and expanding
a mutually enriching relationship after an
enterprise prospect becomes a client.

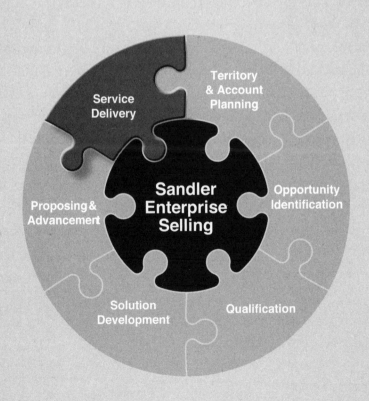

After all the time, money, and effort you invested to pursue the opportunity you just won, it is now time to focus keenly on service excellence in moving forward. (By the way: if you ever lost the business in interactions with this client in the past and won this time around, now is the time to prove the saying: "Failure is a bruise, not a tattoo.") If you communicate effectively during this all-important phase, you will not only position yourself and your organization to make this engagement successful, but also expand the business relationship over time. Too many selling organizations underemphasize the importance of a coordinated, team-driven, information-rich approach to service delivery. This may well be the most important stage of all because it is the stage most likely to reinitiate the enterprise selling cycle as you uncover new opportunities over time. In chapter 24, **Client-centric Satisfaction**, you'll focus on letting the client define success, and you'll learn about a game-changing tool that supports that goal, the Client-centric Satisfaction Tool.

In chapter 25, **Business Requirements Focus**, you'll look at one of the very best ways to serve the client: by making sure everyone on your team understands and stays focused on that shared mission.

In chapter 26, **Team Accelerators**, you'll learn how to build on the work you've already done in account planning to improve your position in the account. You'll also learn how to use Sandler's proprietary Team Storm Tool to conduct powerful brainstorming sessions to drive both service excellence and account expansion.

In chapter 27, you'll learn to use the powerful **Client^2** Tool to exploit new growth opportunities.

Finally, in chapter 28, you'll get some important insights on **Client Retention**.

Why Service Excellence Matters

Consider these facts.

- The average company generates 60–70 percent of its business from existing customers.
- It costs seven times more to acquire a new customer than to retain an existing one.
- As customer relationships mature, profits typically increase and operational expenses decrease.
- The primary reason enterprise customers stay or go is not price but service quality.
- The probability of successfully selling a product/service to an existing customer is more than five times greater than with a prospect.
- A customer is much more likely to defect to a competitor due to a service-related issue as opposed to a price concern.
- The majority of repeat buys made by customers are based on how they feel they've been treated.
- Most customers would pay a premium to get a better level of service.
- A small increase in the customer retention rate can have a huge impact on an organization's profitability.

Everything connects. The more you can expose a prospect organization to the way you will deliver, the more comfortable the prospects become and the more likely you are to win additional business. While the responsibilities of the sales and delivery sides shift once the relationship begins, the sales team must always remain actively engaged in service delivery. Sales team members should want to remain engaged during delivery because the potential to build knowledge, grow, and expand enterprise accounts is so strong.

CHAPTER 24

Client-centric Satisfaction

This chapter can be boiled down to one sentence: Clearly understanding a client's unique success factors increases your chances of successful delivery and account growth.

> **SANDLER ENTERPRISE SELLING RULE**
>
> *Let the client define success.*

It's been said before, but it's worth repeating: you want to have salespeople deeply involved in delivery, building knowledge about the client environment every step of the way. This knowledge of the client's intimate pains and needs increases the potential for client satisfaction—which increases the likelihood that you will sell more.

The fact that the delivery team has been engaged in the pursuit and understands the SES program increases the likelihood that they will be able to help identify new opportunities to grow the account. This continuous, client-centered process of selling and delivery is based on a powerful principle: it's not that the customer is always right, but that the client gets to define success.

Move Beyond Price

Letting the client define success is what allows us to move beyond price.

The initial sales process often finds the prospect focused on issues surrounding price, but that dynamic changes once the contract is signed. Once the agreement is finalized, it's common for a much more nuanced, detailed, and accurate picture of the client's priorities to emerge. You're a partner at this point, and the value you deliver over the long term is more important than the short-term number on the invoice. The information you uncover during your first client-centric satisfaction discussion—and during subsequent meetings—carries immense, long-term strategic importance. But, you have to ask the right questions, and you have to ask them early in the relationship.

Why Your Customer Satisfaction Scores May Be Meaningless—and What to Do about It

Have you ever had the experience of suddenly losing a client who recently gave you passing, or even above-average, marks on a customer-satisfaction survey?

How is that even possible? What would make someone fill out a survey with seemingly positive grades and then turn around and drop you so they could start working with your competition? What kind of communication gap makes that happen, and how do you close it? Those tough questions led to the development of a proprietary Sandler resource, the Client-centric Satisfaction Tool. People have said that the Client-centric Satisfaction Tool is one of the most powerful tools in the SES portfolio. We've even heard the word "revolutionary."

That may not have been a term you expected to hear anyone use in reference to a customer-satisfaction survey. But it's the right word. To understand why this tool is revolutionary, you have to ask: What are most customer-satisfaction processes like?

Typically, they're "one-size-fits-all" surveys. There's a reason many people cringe a little whenever they are asked to fill out one of these forms. They're not interactive. They're a drain on your time. They deliver no real benefit. They're shallow; they're boring, and they're certainly not very effective sales tools. In fact, they're not sales tools at all!

Let's think about what happens in the typical situation. The salesperson closes the deal. Contracts are signed. Service delivery starts. Then the salesperson tells the client that he will return after a certain period of time, maybe six months, to deliver a survey. That survey is supposed to gain the client's perspective on the performance up to that point. But notice that the items on the survey are always created by the selling/delivery firm, and they are not customized to the client.

Now let's fast forward six months. The salesperson drops off the survey, sometimes without any heads-up at all, simply showing up unannounced with the form, leaving it at the front desk, or even e-mailing it.

Let's assume the client actually sees and completes the survey. What happens? The survey contains a list of flattering, cherry-picked criteria like "personal appearance," "charisma," and "fashion sense." Then the client is asked to rate the performance in each of those areas. How valuable is that information? Not very!

After the client fills out a survey like that, who learns from the process? Nobody learns. Not the client. Not the selling organization. No one. The business relationship could be circling the drain. But the preloaded, one-dimensional satisfaction criteria in that survey shed no light on the business relationship.

The Client-centric Satisfaction Tool is different. As the engagement begins, the selling organization's sales and delivery team representatives meet with the client together to discuss customer satisfaction. The Client-centric Satisfaction Tool drives this discussion; it is customized to the client. It sets up an ongoing series of collaborative meetings—not a periodic data dump.

In the initial meeting, the client reviews a list of 12 commonly-cited satisfaction factors. Then the client chooses the five that are the most important to the relationship and the situation and selects weights for each. In addition, the client can do something here that no one-size-fits-all customer survey will allow a client to do. The client can add new factors to the list. If the client wants to make those the most important benchmarks for the relationship going forward, the client can do that.

So not only are the five uniquely important factors for this client identified, but they're ranked in the client's specific priority. This is a treasure trove of client information. Remember, this is for work that is just beginning, not work that has already taken place. You are learning what is important to your client at the beginning of the relationship. Think of how powerful that is.

You use the tool to record everything you uncover during the interview about this specific client—the clear success criteria for the emerging relationship. Then you get ready for the follow-up meeting when your service delivery performance will be judged against the client's specific criteria.

Closely consider Figure 24.1. Can you see why you don't just drop this off at the front desk and tell the client to fill it out? The Client-centric Satisfaction Tool meeting is an important collaborative discussion—a strategic interchange. It has to take place face-to-face or voice-to-voice. This meeting is a critical interviewing and project-launch milestone. You pose a whole lot of good questions, face-to-face, and you generate a lot of in-depth answers. The information that results is a competitive gold mine.

Who gets smarter during this survey-completion session? You might be tempted to say that it's the sales team, and you wouldn't be wrong. But actually, it's not just the sales team. Remember, the delivery team is in on this meeting as well. So both sales and delivery get into alignment as a team about what's most important to this brand-new client. Frankly, the client learns as well. The client learns a lot about this new

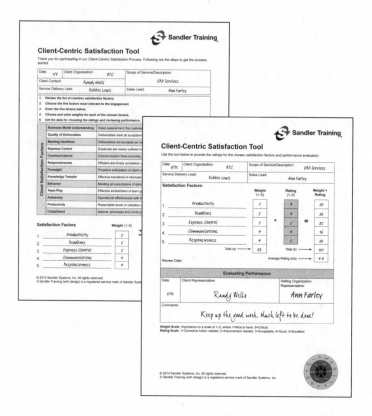

partner, and about how much that partner cares about understanding what matters most to the client. How do you think that makes the client feel?

What happens after the initial meeting? You explain to the new client that you're going to come back and continue the process of evaluating how you did against the benchmarks you've set up. You identify what's important for the future. You do this on a regular basis, ideally every three to six months. This launches a relationship that's based on solid information, not empty generic surveys. Of course, you are in contact and in communication with the client throughout service delivery.

Use the Customer-centric Satisfaction Tool, and you can make fundamental changes in your program that directly affect the client's most important issues. Without that information, you're probably going in the wrong direction. You might never have known the customer's most important issues, or you might not have known in time to make a difference. You might just lose the business—even though your contact gave you 10 out of 10 for charisma and fashion sense.

Sandler's proprietary Client-centric Satisfaction Tool gives a crystal-clear picture of a client's motivations, needs, and pains that positions you to deliver successfully and earn the right to sell more.

A True Story

Lorrie Evans, a sales rep with the interestingly named Modi-Fleet, won a deal providing fleet vehicle services to a new client—let's call them *MotoServOne*. When she won the business, she informed Kurt Nolan, her key MotoServOne client contact, that she would provide a customer satisfaction survey six months after the business relationship started, and that Kurt would fill it out to grade Modi-Fleet's performance.

Six months passed and Lorrie e-mailed Kurt the survey, as promised. He reviewed the preset categories and gave Modi-Fleet passing grades in all four areas they had identified. Two weeks later, Lorrie received a letter from Kurt invoking their 60-day cancellation clause to end the contract. Lorrie sent Kurt an e-mail, indicating her surprise with the cancellation due the passing grades he had provided just a short time ago. Kurt responded by sharing that their high dissatisfaction level was related to Modi-Fleet's inability to service MotoServOne's remote locations, something that was very important to Kurt and his team—one of their key initiatives had been upgrading the levels of support to their outlying locations. Kurt had shared with Modi-Fleet's service teams that they were unhappy about the issue, but Kurt had seen no evidence that the issue was receiving any attention. Nothing on Modi-Fleet's generic customer satisfaction survey pointed to the issue, so he simply filled it out, grading the preset criteria. Kurt further shared that they had contracted with Modi-Fleet's largest competitor on a three-year deal for their future business.

Two Key Client-centric Satisfaction Tool Events: Initiation and Rating

1. **Initiation:** At the start of the engagement, the client identifies criteria from a list of suggestions and weights these, based on their relative importance.
2. **Rating:** At the conclusion of a mutually-agreed-upon time frame, the client provides actual ratings for the previously chosen criteria. At this point, you schedule the next meeting with the client.

With the Client-centric Satisfaction Tool, you can make fundamental changes in your program that directly affect the client's most important issues. This tool, if you use it correctly, maximizes the probability of delivery success. Gaining a view into how the new client thinks and defines success gives you critical insights to share with the delivery team. Using what you learn from the client, you can amend your focus, if need be, in order to be in alignment with the client's view of success.

This tool also provides you with a road map to winning new business. In fact, each new opportunity gives you the chance to learn even more valuable information about your client—information that will help you to deliver successfully and win more business.

If you schedule regular client-centric satisfaction sessions, and you follow up appropriately, you will be viewed as a partner who delivers, and you'll have information about the client's priorities that your competitors simply do not have. That translates into an enduring competitive advantage.

CHAPTER 25

Business Requirements Focus

In the ideal enterprise pursuit and proposal process, the client's business requirements are always clearly understood and top of mind for everyone in the selling organization. In the real world, despite everyone's best efforts, the team members with direct-selling responsibility tend to be the people who focus most closely on this.

After an engagement has been won and delivery is underway, the business requirements can often become obscured. The task orientation and work breakdown structure of client service can lead to the creation of delivery silos, with the result that the "big picture" becomes blurred. Delivery team members come and go, and the time frame and life cycle of the engagement can dull your clear understanding of even the most fundamental themes of the relationship.

You can be certain, though, that the clients remember their overall goals—and you, as the service provider, need to ensure that the sales and delivery teams make a conscious effort to keep those goals in mind. If the goals are forgotten or overlooked, client satisfaction and account expansion will be in jeopardy. These goals are the reason you are here. It is your job to make sure they remain visible and fresh in everyone's mind.

SANDLER ENTERPRISE SELLING RULE

Serve the client by understanding the mission.

Business Requirements, Revisited

You've seen this list before, but it is here again to remind you that it's your job to use it as a conversation starter, over and over again, throughout the service-delivery process, with as many internal team members as possible. If you ever begin to think you've covered this with the internal team, that's a sign that you should review the items on this list again.

Following, you'll find 10 critical business requirements you will need to double check as part of the service delivery team discussion.

1. The problem or pain to be addressed
2. The fundamental aspects of the new capability that is needed
3. Who the users will be and how they will use the new capability

4. How this new capability will best address the problem and pain
5. The benefits that will result
6. When the new capability is needed
7. The dependencies that need to be understood
8. The risks in this initiative
9. What is in and out of the scope of the initiative
10. The key assumptions being made

Staying focused on the business requirements allows you to deliver on the client's expectations.

Ignoring the business requirements—even as a result of being busy, even when you lack technical knowledge that connects to the solution and you think you don't belong in the conversation, even when your intentions are entirely good—diminishes your chances of meeting or exceeding the client's expectations.

Gather the Team

To help keep the focus on business requirements as sharp as possible, gather the team after you win the business and review the 10 critical business requirements focus areas. Yes, they were touched on in Stage Four in the chapter titled "Refine the Position." It was easy to focus on the business requirements like a laser beam then, wasn't it? Why? Because you wanted to win the business.

Well, you did just that. But you need to remain focused on them if you want to keep and grow the business.

Think of a key client initiative in which you're currently involved. Looking over the list again, what jumps out at you as most important for this specific engagement? Is remembering the initial pain important? Why? Are the initial pain points important to the actual users of your product or service? Are they engaged with you? What about the risks that you faced initially? Are you still keeping a lookout for them, or are you so splintered in your service approach that they are not even being charted? These are all important questions.

CHAPTER 26

Team Accelerators

You've won the business, and you clearly understand the critical customized success factors. Your team is focused on delivery excellence, and the client's all-important business requirements are front and center.

The single most important thing that has to happen now is for "salespeople" and "delivery people" to drop their labels. There is only one team now, and the members of that team have to work together to drive client satisfaction and grow the account.

Your job is to improve the position in the account that's just been won. This is the point at which true, ongoing collaboration between the sales side and the delivery side becomes essential for success. The tools in this chapter will actively support that goal.

These tools are called "team accelerators" for a reason—they are designed to drive accelerated growth through team collaboration on behalf of the client. Make no mistake: That's the only reliable way to expand enterprise accounts—to collaborate.

BEYOND SERVICE AND DELIVERY

Not only are the two teams equally important—they're really one team.

Especially for people on the delivery side, it's natural to become deeply involved in client service issues. But sometimes that involvement comes at the expense of communication with the client and with team members on the sales side. The two proprietary Sandler tools coming up next, Growth Account Booster and Team Storm, are designed to provide for easy facilitation of team collaboration.

The kind of teamwork discussed here allows everyone to lift their heads out of the weeds and focus on account growth. These tools help resolve delivery issues quickly and proactively, which is in everyone's best interests. Of course, in solving delivery problems, you are also increasing the likelihood that you'll grow the account.

Growth Account Booster, Revisited

The first tool focused on in team accelerators is the Growth Account Booster Tool. You first reviewed the Growth Account Booster in Stage One: Territory & Account Planning. In that stage, the Growth Account Booster provided the account planning platform for the key accounts you identified as a result of your territory planning process. Account planning, of course, is a dynamic process providing a framework for account success throughout the sales and relationship cycles. Account planning is not a one-time event, but a vehicle that is continually refreshed to update the significant actions to be taken to achieve advances necessary to win enterprise business.

Now, in the Service Delivery stage, the business relationship is active and the prospect is the client. Every day serving the client builds trust, experience, and a firsthand understanding of client needs and pains. This evolving picture makes the continued use of the Growth Account Booster Tool in the now-active relationship much more meaningful. The selling and delivery teams convened in the first Growth Account Booster session, typically facilitated by the sales lead, will now consist of some old and new faces. The results of the collaboration driven by the process can go a long way to maximize client satisfaction and account growth.

Team Storm

Next to explore is the second Team Accelerator, the Team Storm Tool. The operative word there is *team*.

At this point, you should know what to say if someone were to ask you, "Which is more important once you close the deal—the selling team or the delivery team?" As has been emphasized repeatedly, the delivery team should be partnered in the selling process, and the sales team should be partnered in delivery. The correct answer is that there is only one team.

That answer leads to an important question. Now that you know that you're supposed to be operating as one team, whose problem is it when there are sudden issues that come up in serving the client? Is that a service problem or a delivery problem?

Of course, that's a trick question, too. Both service and delivery must work together to deal with the challenges and opportunities that present themselves in the dynamic client relationship.

What you need, then, is a tool that will help everyone come together to deal with issues in a way that serves the client and the selling organization. That's what's coming up next—a tool that does just that. It's called the Team Storm Tool (Figure 26.1). That's storm as in brainstorm!

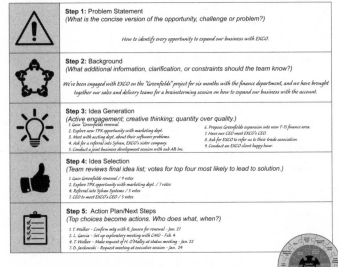

Team Storm, a tool for effectively and quickly addressing issues, may be the most powerful selling-side collaboration tool of all. It works because it allows all the team members' time to be used as cost-effectively as possible. Team Storm sessions are rapid events. You get involved, generate action items and move on with the rest of the day.

TEAM STORM SESSIONS MOVE FAST

This is not your grandfather's meeting.

Team Storm delivers effective action items that everyone owns and can implement, and it does so in a hurry. The key to making that happen is participation. This is a proven structure for a direct, participatory conversation that brings together team members who share the same vested interest in a structure that supports dynamic group participation. (That means no monologues allowed.) Without that type of structure, what happens? Confusion and frustration, wasted time, no progress, unclear follow up and a lack of clear next steps for improving the relationship with the client.

Everyone has been there at one point or another. Team Storm is the selling organization's vaccination against those outcomes.

Let's look closely now at how this proprietary Sandler tool works.

Team Storm and the Art of Managing Change

Each Team Storm discussion is driven by a single objective, usually client-driven and time-sensitive. Enterprise accounts are incredibly dynamic, and a delivery organization's ability to manage change is a critical survival skill. You need to be nimble and agile in addressing situations so that, as a team, you can move forward as quickly as possible and in a seamless manner.

Organizations that constantly get caught up in lengthy analyses and long meetings to address situations simply don't survive in the enterprise world. The pace of the game is just too fast. Effective collaboration and rapid group brainstorming are critical tools for organizations dedicated to serving enterprise clients.

With Team Storm, you can move your organization toward a new level of mastery in that area.

Three Things to Remember About Team Storm

First and foremost, Team Storm is a **rapid decision-making tool.** That's because issues that come up in the enterprise selling world usually require a quick response. If people ever start to think that the meeting is dragging on, you're doing it wrong. Second, as noted above, successful Team Storm sessions thrive on **participation.** For the session to work, the facilitator must tactfully and good-naturedly elicit feedback from all members of the team. Last but not least is the delivery mode. This is a **high-touch, low-tech tool.** You shouldn't run this meeting with a spreadsheet or a PowerPoint deck. It's meant to be conducted with old-school tools—flip charts and markers.

Know When to Use Team Storm

Team Storm is not for every situation.

It's for when you need fast action and fast results on one specific issue that everyone knows about going into the meeting.

It's for when you have the right people in the room. That means people with background, interest, and motivation to address the issue—people who are invested, and like being invested, in the task of serving enterprise clients.

It's for when you need accountability. Unlike some team meeting processes you may have done before where accountability slips through the cracks, accountability is rock solid in Team Storm. With this tool, the whole is greater than the sum of its parts.

Who's Who?

Team Storm has a very simple organizational chart. First there's the facilitator role. The facilitator is the true leader, driving the activities. The facilitator directs the process and helps develop the team's ideas. Often participants need some support with this one. Facilitators motivate, drive forward motion, and keep the team focused. This is an active role, calling for real leadership, coaching, and guidance to keep the focus and ensure the effectiveness of the process.

Team members make up the rest of the organizational chart. They work to address issues and to provide ideas, suggestions, and builds—attachments to another person's idea. This promotes an environment of seeking improvement, participating, listening, keeping an open mind, and being encouraging to your teammates. If this is missing, the Team Storm session won't deliver positive results.

The Five Steps of a Team Storm Meeting

There are five steps for a good Team Storm meeting: problem statement, background, idea generation, idea selection, and action plan next steps. Let's look at each of them in detail.

Step One: Problem Statement

This is the initial statement of the opportunity, the challenge or the problem being faced by the group. It is delivered in a simple, clear headline, not in a rambling format. To foster constructive discussion, the problem statement is delivered via action orientation, preceded by the words "how to."

Step Two: Background

This involves providing the information and clarifications that might be needed to understand the problem. Typically, since your team members are already invested, this is not a lengthy session. Provide a quick context check, get everybody on the same page, and move on.

Step Three: Idea Generation

This is the marrow of Team Storm. Hands go up, ideas are shared, and the problem statement is addressed. The ideas go up on the flip-chart sheets, which can cover the walls if you use sheets with adhesive. This is active engagement. Look for a lot of creative thinking in step three. The key is to get a lot of ideas out there, as quickly as possible.

Step Four: Idea Selection

This step is where the team votes on the list of ideas as they have been formulated and consolidated by the facilitator. The ideas that received the most votes are taken to the next step.

Step Five: Action Plan/Next Step

This step is where the facilitator leads a conclusive discussion of who's going to do what and when. Obviously, the stronger and more time-driven the commitments are in step five, the better the chance of success in resolving the problem. The accountable parties report back to the team, typically via electronic means.

That's the Team Storm session in a nutshell. Like the tool itself, it's short but sweet.

Team Storm is not just for emergencies. It's for whenever you have a group problem to solve and you need fast action and quick practical results. For instance, at a time when there are no pressing client-focused problems to address, you might choose objectives like these.

- How to serve Client X more effectively
- How to take advantage of every opportunity to serve Client X
- How to anticipate the future needs of Client X
- How to identify the actions needed to ensure a multi-year (five-plus) relationship with Client X
- How to communicate more effectively as a team in serving Client X
- How to identify specific actions that will increase Client X's satisfaction

CHAPTER 27

Client²

This book has focused on lots of different ways to achieve and sustain competitive advantage by means of winning or keeping an initial piece of enterprise business. Now it's time to focus on the growth potential that is the hallmark of enterprise accounts. It's time to think about gaining a competitive advantage by treating each enterprise client as a market unto itself.

SANDLER ENTERPRISE SELLING RULE

*There is no better time to win business
than after you've won business.*

Bloom Where You're Planted

Enterprise accounts are deep and wide with connections and touch points across a vast ecosystem of opportunity.

As mentioned above, each enterprise client is a marketplace in and of itself, deserving similar focus and energy to that which you devote to your territory marketplace. The Client^2 process enables you to grow these enterprise client marketplaces by following a logical and growth-oriented framework. This is what is meant when salespeople are told, "Bloom where you're planted." An enterprise account presents many opportunities for growth, within and beyond the initial engagement. Of course, you want to win as many of those opportunities as possible.

Let's say you've just won the business and your initial engagement is kicking off. At the start of an enterprise business relationship, the focus is always on delivery excellence, and rightfully so. At the same time, this very focus on service excellence presents great opportunities to sell more.

These great opportunities are the focus of the Client^2 Tool's five key areas: organic growth, partnerships and alliances, family tree, alumni, and customer's customer.

Organic growth is the first focus area and the one that selling organizations are most likely to focus on, at least to some degree. This involves the extension and/or the renewal of the current business and also expansion into other groups, divisions, or departments of the enterprise client. The focus should also be on identifying client teams and needs that other products and services in your portfolio can address. So this first part of Client^2 is all about going deep and wide with the client and across your offerings portfolio. When you think about organic growth, think about:

- Project renewal/extension
- Project expansion
- Other client areas
- Other client locations
- Your other products and services

Partnerships and alliances is the next part of the model. An enterprise account will expose you to business, channel, and alliance partners whose relationships with your firm can lead to significant new opportunities within and beyond the current client. Treat these partner organizations like clients and get to know them well—their business models, their offerings, their culture, and so on. Understanding partnerships and alliances leads to collaboration—which leads to business. These relationships, of course, demand some analysis and discretion. Think before you act. When you think about partnerships and alliances, think about:

- Partners as "marketplaces"
- Partners' needs and pains
- Joint selling
- Joint delivery
- "Live" deals
- Relationships at executive levels

Family tree, the next element of Client², is a slice of the enterprise "pie" too often ignored or overlooked. The quality work that you do in serving the client should add warmth and some level of receptivity with other members of the client's family as well. Seeking your client's advocacy and referral is a natural thing when it comes to subsidiaries, sister companies, the parent company, holding company partners, consortium members, and so on. Make sure you consider and research them all. Some companies with no obvious connection operate under the same corporate umbrella: GEICO and Dairy Queen, for instance, are both owned by Berkshire-Hathaway. There are no guarantees, of course, but blood is thicker than water. Working the client's family tree can and does pay off. When you think about this part of the Client^2 model, think about:

- Sister companies
- Subsidiaries
- Parents
- Client's business partners
- Industry/trade groups

The **alumni** category is all about following individual client contacts to new firms if they leave the client organization and being creative and innovative in so doing. You should also work backwards by seeking client referrals into their former employers, where their opinion may still carry weight. Alumni of your client organization who predated your involvement may still give great credence to partners chosen by their previous employer. With discretion, reviewing a client contact's LinkedIn network can unearth great opportunities to seek connections into new firms where you could win business. Don't forget alumni of business partners as well. As previously mentioned, good sense, respect, and due diligence should prevail here. When you think about this part of the Client^2 model, think about:

- Client alumni in prospect firms
- Partner alumni in prospect firms
- Client contacts in prospect firms
- Client alumni as hires or subcontractors

That brings us to the final Client^2 focus area, the **customer's customer**. In working with an enterprise client, you will often be exposed to their actual customers. These people are likely to be involved with you, as your delivery work may deliver direct value to them—in what is known as a "connected benefit." Relationships arising in this category can be fruitful opportunities for enterprise selling—but be very careful. You must always carry yourself professionally. Especially in this area, use discretion, and be aware that client concurrence prior to any contact is absolutely critical. Include professional organizations and trade boards in this category because they, too, are close to the client you serve and often deliver referrals that are equally close to your key contacts. When you think about this part of the Client^2 model, think about:

- Client's customers with whom you have become familiar
- "Connected benefit" sources

A True Story

A national commercial real estate management firm—we'll call them *Servacast Company*—has a standard practice of viewing every client as a marketplace unto itself. In other words, they have built a clear process for seeking new business opportunities as offshoots from business that they have already won. A great enterprise success story comes from their Atlanta office. There, they won the local office business of a regional janitorial services firm, and they leased them 4,200 square feet of space in nearby Dunwoody. In working with this local client, Servacast worked the process they always follow in seeking organic growth. They identified that the client was part of a larger operation—a regional janitorial services firm headquartered in Charlotte with seven offices in the southeast. The Dunwoody client was quite pleased with Servacast's service and provided an entree into a discussion with the corporate headquarters in Charlotte.

Servacast ultimately won the business for all seven regional operational offices, leasing each of them new offices.

It gets better. As part of the Servacast process of viewing each client as a marketplace, they worked the family tree concept and identified that the Charlotte headquarters was a subsidiary of a $1.2 billion firm with companies providing temporary contract services not only in the janitorial space but also in food services, paralegal, and event management. As Charlotte was also quite happy with the service provided to them by Servacast, the contact there facilitated an introduction to the corporate parent. Ultimately an agreement was reached and was signed for Servacast to serve all 48 North American locations of the corporate parent in the four different verticals that they serve.

Now Is the Time

There really is no better time to win business than after you've won business. Client^2 provides the guidance to help identify many new opportunity areas. It is not an event—it's a mind-set. To enter that mind-set, just ask yourself a simple question, "What have I done today to grow this client?"

CHAPTER 28

Client Retention

S atisfying, growing, and retaining enterprise clients takes on an importance akin to that of survival for selling organizations. The following are 10 key principles to keep in mind for effective client retention during Stage Six: Service Delivery.

Client Retention

The 10 key principles of client retention:

1. Do what you say you'll do.
2. Know your client and stay updated.
3. Communicate constantly.
4. Deliver value.
5. Listen internally and externally.
6. Sell and deliver as a team.
7. Anticipate the next move that best serves the client.

8. Be proactive in serving.
9. Care.
10. Be in the game for the long term.

No one of these 10 principles is more important than any other, but if they had to be boiled down to a single sentence, it would have to be that first commandment.

SANDLER ENTERPRISE SELLING PRINCIPLE

Do what you say you'll do.

Client retention is a mindset, a mantra, and your charter. It's fitting that this book ends here because the foundation principle of SES is that the process never ends.

Client retention is really an obligation to yourself, your firm, and all of its stakeholders to continue delivering value. Most importantly, though, this is an obligation you have to the client who made a conscious decision to choose you as a partner. Not only should you not take that lightly, but your every action should be focused on keeping that partnership alive and well for the long haul.

Follow through on your commitments and you'll earn the right to expand the enterprise relationship over time.

Epilogue

Winning, growing, and keeping enterprise accounts are challenging objectives that demand the best of the sales and delivery teams and the organization as a whole.

The Sandler Enterprise Selling program is uniquely positioned to help you achieve those goals. It will guide you to results in each of the six key areas you have now studied.

- Your efforts in setting a strong baseline in Territory & Account Planning will not only support all of your client-related activities but also maximize the likelihood that you pursue only the right clients and deals. This essential prework helps ensure that your hit rates and account growth results are robust.
- Following the Opportunity Identification process will help you streamline your efforts through focused tools and practical concepts that make seeking specific enterprise opportunities easier, more targeted, and more efficient.
- Sandler Enterprise Selling's Qualification stage will guide your organization's teaming activities to provide clarity and confidence for the deals that you pursue.

- In the Solution Development stage, you will craft win/win solutions that have a high probability of closing.
- The Proposing & Advancement stage is where you either win or learn—and begin to capitalize on the significant opportunities presented within each of those outcomes.
- As you transition to client service and relationship management in the Service Delivery stage, you'll make client satisfaction the first priority, expand the relationship over time, and cultivate the mindset that each enterprise client is a marketplace unto itself. This mind-set positions both you and the client to grow and prosper.

Consistent focus on superior service is the key to driving client satisfaction and retention over time, ensuring a continuous process of successful selling and delivery in long-term business relationships, and unleashing a steady stream of entirely new opportunities.

This is the world of winning, growing, and keeping enterprise accounts. When navigated with care, attention, and commitment, that world can be the setting for a journey of success that does not end.

ONE LAST QUOTE

*"Your satisfied customers are your
brand's best ambassador."*

—Kim Bookman, in "Top Boosting Sales Tips for Small Business Owners"
(Article posted November 12, 2014, atwww.blogher.com
/top-boosting-sales-tips-small-business-owners)

What's your brand? Ideally, it's your happiest client. Whatever you need to do to get there, within the bounds of ethics, the law, and good business practices, that's where you want to be.

That's where we all want to be—thinking about what we need to do to keep our enterprise clients happy over the long term. Why? Because happy clients are the best marketing campaign of all. Sandler Enterprise Selling is there to help you and support you as you launch and sustain that campaign.

LET'S CONNECT ON LINKEDIN!

http://bit.ly/ses_linkedin

*This link will take you to LinkedIn's Sandler
Enterprise Selling Group. Join the discussion!*

Index

Sandler Enterprise Selling
includes a complimentary seminar!

Take this opportunity to personally experience the non-traditional sales training and reinforcement coaching that has been recognized internationally for decades.

Companies in the Fortune 1000 as well as thousands of small- to medium-sized businesses choose Sandler Training for sales, leadership, management, and a wealth of other skill-building programs. Now, it's your turn, and it's free!

You'll learn the latest practical, tactical, feet-in-the-street sales methods directly from your neighborhood Sandler trainers! They're knowledgeable, friendly, and informed about your local selling environment.

Here's how you redeem YOUR FREE SEMINAR invitation.

1. Go to www.Sandler.com and click on the LOCATE A TRAINING CENTER button (upper right corner).
2. Select your location from the drop-down menus.
3. Review the list of all the Sandler trainers in your area.
4. Call your local Sandler trainer, mention *Sandler Enterprise Selling,* and reserve your place at the next seminar!